TIGERS
CONFIDENTIAL

TIGERS
CONFIDENTIAL

THE UNTOLD INSIDE STORY
OF THE 2008 SEASON

Andy Van Slyke
with Jim Hawkins

TRIUMPH
BOOKS

Triumph Books and colophon are registered trademarks of Random House, Inc.

Library of Congress Cataloging-in-Publication Data

Slyke, Andy Van.
  Tigers confidential : the untold inside story of the 2008 season / Andy Van Slyke with Jim Hawkins.
     p. cm.
  ISBN 978-1-60078-168-1
  1. Detroit Tigers (Baseball team)—History—21st century. I. Hawkins, Jim. II. Title.
  GV875.D6S6 2009
  796.357'640977434—dc22

                         2008055267

This book is available in quantity at special discounts for your group or organization. For further information, contact:

Triumph Books
542 South Dearborn Street
Suite 750
Chicago, Illinois 60605
(312) 939-3330
Fax (312) 663-3557

Printed in U.S.A.
ISBN: 978-1-60078-168-1
Page production by Patricia Frey
Photos courtesy of Getty Images unless otherwise indicated.

To the Detroit Tigers organization and fans. You all make me proud to wear the Tigers uniform.

—Andy Van Slyke

To Jack, Tabitha, and Bethany, who make every year a championship year.

—Jim Hawkins

Contents

"I'm excited. I think we're all excited. But there is no perfect club out there. Perfect clubs don't exist. I don't care who you are, you always lose games in baseball."

—Dave Dombrowski,
Detroit Tigers president/general manager

"This is the best lineup I've ever had, top to bottom, there's no question about that. The only loser in this thing could be me. If we don't win, I'll be in Lima, Ohio, picking up stuff with the chickens."

—Jim Leyland,
Detroit Tigers manager

Chapter 1

THE OFF-SEASON

"What a Great Addition for Us!"

DECEMBER 4, 2007

NASHVILLE, TN

Today's show-stopping, baseball-shaking, blockbuster trade with the Florida Marlins caught everyone, including the Detroit Tigers' brass, by surprise.

And it immediately catapulted the Tigers into the role of preseason favorites to win the Central Division title, the American League pennant, and, in the minds of many, even the World Series.

Literally overnight, the Tigers, injured underachievers in 2007, became the talk of baseball and, for the first time in more than two decades, the Team to Beat.

Yesterday morning, in a quiet corner of one of the many lobbies of the sprawling 40-acre Opryland Resort, with its waterfalls, atriums, bridges, gift

In a blockbuster, eight-player trade with the Florida Marlins that caught the baseball world by surprise, the Tigers acquired young superstar Miguel Cabrera (right) and former 22-game winner Dontrelle Willis, overnight making the Tigers the team to beat in the American League.

shops, and endless hallways, Jim Leyland, the Tigers' crusty manager, admitted the team had come to baseball's annual winter convention intent on doing nothing more dramatic than maybe "tweaking" things here and there.

Dave Dombrowski, the team's president and general manager, said basically the same thing when he met with a handful of Detroit writers later the same day.

The Tigers were set for the 2008 season, content to sit back and watch baseball's other teams worry about filling holes in their rosters and shedding superfluous salaries.

For the Tigers, who surprised the baseball world by advancing to the World Series in 2006—the once-proud franchise's first winning season after a dozen consecutive forlorn summers under .500—it was definitely going to be a boring week.

"I'm down here to have a few glasses of wine and see a few friends," Leyland joked that evening, firing up another Marlboro outside in the parking lot, one of the few places around the 2,881-room Opryland Hotel where the Tigers manager's second-favorite pastime—smoking—was permitted.

For 106 years, baseball's executives on both the major- and minor-league levels have gathered each off-season to discuss the business of the Grand Old Game and, more importantly, to try to swap players.

Rumors were rampant that Minnesota Twins ace pitcher Johan Santana, a two-time Cy Young Award winner, and Florida's undercelebrated Miguel Cabrera, one of the most formidable young sluggers in the game, would be on the trading block this week.

However, none of the many hypothetical scenarios swirling around those two superstars, or others, involved the Detroit Tigers.

Parting with the pride of the Tigers' farm system, either pitcher Andrew Miller or outfielder Cameron Maybin—let alone both of them—was the furthest thing from anyone's mind.

Those two kids, both of whom debuted with the Tigers during the 2007 season, with mixed results, were assumed to be as untouchable as Eliot Ness.

Having already moved Carlos Guillen to first base to ease the stress on his aching knees; having acquired veteran Edgar Renteria to replace Guillen at shortstop and Jacque Jones to platoon in left field; having re-signed future Hall of Famer Pudge Rodriguez to again be their every-day catcher, Todd Jones to be their closer, and Kenny Rogers to be one of their starting pitchers, the Tigers were ready for 2008.

Or so they thought.

Then, at 7:00 AM this morning, the telephone rang in Dave Dombrowski's swank sixth-floor suite.

On the other end of the line at that early hour was Larry Beinfest, president of the cash-strapped Florida Marlins, offering to swap the All-Star slugger Cabrera and former 22-game winner Dontrelle Willis for prize Tigers prospects Cameron Maybin and Andrew Miller, plus four other players, none of whom figured prominently in the team's plans for the immediate future.

Members of the Tigers' front office were stunned.

Following a mandatory general managers' meeting this morning, an anxious Dombrowski summoned Jim Leyland along with all of the Tigers' executives, scouts, and minor-league officials to his suite.

Then Dave locked the door.

"All I want is your opinion on whether you would make this deal or not," Dombrowski told his staff, most of them handpicked by the Tigers' CEO after he was given almost total control of the floundering franchise in 2002. "Don't get into the financing. I'll worry about the financing."

"That room was intense," Jim Leyland admitted later. "I usually don't get too excited about trades or free-agent signings. But I was a little shook up. I did a lot of pacing."

One by one, each man in the room spoke his piece.

"It was unanimous: 'Let's do it,'" Leyland said.

"This wasn't a no-brainer," the Tigers manager added. "This was a brainer."

Late this afternoon, Dombrowski phoned Tigers owner Mike Ilitch at his home to let him know—in terms of both dollars and talent—exactly what it would take to put Miguel Cabrera and Dontrelle Willis into uniforms bearing the Olde English *D*.

After all, given the big bucks involved, a deal of this magnitude is not made without the blessing of the boss.

"Are you sitting down?" Dombrowski asked Ilitch, who made his fortune peddling Little Caesars pizza pies.

The reclusive 78-year-old Tigers owner laughed.

When Dombrowski laid out the details of the proposed trade with the Marlins, Ilitch—who played a prominent role in the earlier signings of free agents Pudge Rodriguez and Magglio Ordonez, key cogs in the Tigers' renaissance, and who had recently urged Dombrowski to explore the possibility of acquiring Cabrera—simply said, "Wow!"

"It hit him out of the blue," Dombrowski said later. "He was thrilled."

A world championship was at the top of Ilitch's Bucket List.

The Tigers were going all-in.

With Ilitch's backing, Dombrowski phoned the Marlins to say they had a deal—a scant 19 hours after the two teams had first discussed such a trade in the most elementary, exploratory terms late last night.

However, there was one hitch. Before the trade could become official, the Tigers and Marlins had to exchange and review medical reports on each of the eight players involved in the deal. Even with the modern-day efficiency of the Internet, emails, and fax machines, that process takes time.

Worried that word might leak out and jeopardize the deal, the Tigers officials were sequestered in Dombrowski's suite, sworn to secrecy, and ordered to stay put.

"It was like walking by the tree the day before Christmas and seeing all those presents—and your mom and dad won't let you open any of them," a grinning Leyland admitted later.

I first became convinced that the rumors of a major trade involving the Tigers and Marlins that had been whispered throughout the hotel since midday were true when I approached Dombrowski's suite for his scheduled press briefing late this afternoon and found Rob Matwick, the Tigers' vice president of communications, standing guard outside the door.

"The meeting has been canceled," Matwick said cryptically.

I headed back to the media workroom, phoned my newspaper, *The Oakland Press*, with an update and immediately began writing the story that I had been piecing together since noon.

I have been in this business since 1966 and covered my first winter meetings in 1970, but I sensed this trade.

Upstairs, in Dombrowski's suite, the Tigers ordered pizza for the entire staff. With Dombrowski's permission, Leyland slipped out for a much-needed cigarette and a late-night dinner with his close friend, St. Louis Cardinals manager Tony La Russa.

But other than that, until the blockbuster became official early the following day, the Tigers execs were rarely allowed to leave the room except to sleep. Loose lips sink ships.

"There was a big sigh of relief when Dave finally gave us the thumbs-up that the deal was done," Leyland admitted.

"You know," the Tigers manager added softly, as if somehow the thought had just crept into his mind after 31 nerve-wracking hours, "this really is a big deal. This is huge. It's all been mind-boggling.

"I had no idea something like this was going to happen. This is probably the most shocked I've ever been at any winter meetings. I've had a headache for two days.

"Dave [Dombrowski] really showed me something, the way he stepped up to the plate," Leyland declared.

"I think I'm a pretty aggressive manager. I pull some strings in the dugout. But I would never have been able to pull the trigger on this trade. That took some guts, man. I would have been a nervous wreck."

The unexpected addition of the boyish, underappreciated Miguel Cabrera, with his unlimited potential, and the effervescent Dontrelle Willis, with his funky wind-up, instantly propelled the Tigers into the baseball spotlight.

The Tigers haven't had a slugger of Cabrera's caliber and potential since young Hank Greenberg emerged in the 1930s.

This was the Tigers' biggest deal since the famous Denny McLain heist 37 years earlier.

Since their disappointing showing in the 2006 World Series, the Tigers have added a designated hitter (Gary Sheffield), a shortstop (Renteria), a third baseman (Cabrera), and a left-handed starting pitcher (Willis)—all of them All-Stars in seasons past—all without giving up a single player who had spent so much as one full season in the major leagues.

That's quite a tribute to Dombrowski's ability to wheel and deal.

Only after the trade was announced did Dombrowski reveal the story of how the stunning deal unfolded, beginning with a casual early-evening phone call from Mike Ilitch, the normally hands-off owner, to Dombrowski's home two days before Thanksgiving.

The fact that it was, incredibly, the first time in Dombrowski's six years as the Tigers' CEO that Ilitch had ever phoned him at home only added to the drama.

"I keep reading this guy Miguel Cabrera's name in the paper," Ilitch told Dombrowski. "Do we have any interest in him?"

"Yes, we do," Dombrowski replied, never imagining anything might come of the whimsical conversation.

Dombrowski, in fact, already knew Miguel Cabrera better than most. It was Dombrowski, then the general manager of the Florida Marlins, who had signed Cabrera to his first professional contract in 1999.

"It seems like he would be a great player for us," Ilitch said.

"Yeah, he would be," Dombrowski agreed, smiling to himself at the idea, no matter how far-fetched.

What team wouldn't want a young slugger of Cabrera's ability in its lineup?

"Maybe it's something we could do," Ilitch suggested. "Maybe we can work something out."

"We'll see," Dombrowski said.

Then both men hung up.

"I didn't think it was realistic," Dombrowski admitted after the dream had become a reality.

Nevertheless, in baseball as in any business, a smart executive never ignores a suggestion from his boss.

It was no secret that Cabrera was available—for the right price. Everyone at this winter's meetings had heard that. And late yesterday evening, Dombrowski instructed his right-hand man, Tigers assistant GM Al Avila, to phone the Florida Marlins to find out exactly what they might be looking for in exchange for Cabrera.

The two teams bounced some preliminary names back and forth, but Dombrowski remained skeptical. Such a trade still seemed like a pipe dream. The Tigers had no intention of parting with either Cameron Maybin or Andrew Miller, who were considered to be the future of the franchise. And they certainly would not part with both of them.

Still, Dombrowski has been in baseball long enough to know you never say never.

"I told our people, 'We're going to be open-minded, we're going to throw some things out there and see if we can get better,'" the Tigers GM revealed later.

"Somebody was going to get him [Cabrera]," the often-blunt Leyland pointed out in a futile effort to dodge the barrage of premature pennant predictions that he knew were sure to follow. "What were we supposed to do, wait around for somebody else to grab him?"

Then, shaking his head in amazement at the suddenness of it all, Leyland admitted, "A month or so ago, we were a much different club."

Suddenly, the Tigers were much, much better.

For me, it was eerily similar to the scenario that had unfolded 37 years earlier when, on a flight to the 1970 World Series, Bob Short, the starstruck owner of the Washington Senators, handed a neatly folded sheet of paper to then-Tigers general manager Jim Campbell, who was seated across the aisle of the airplane.

On it, Short had written four names: Senators pitchers Joe Coleman and Jim Hannan, shortstop Eddie Brinkman, and third baseman Aurelio Rodriguez.

All that Short wanted from the Tigers in return were washed-up Denny McLain, over-the-hill third baseman Don Wert, and prospects Elliott Maddox and Norm McRae.

Campbell later confessed it was all he could do not to jump right out of his seat. Today, Dave Dombrowski understood how his deceased predecessor felt. Gifts like this fall into a team's lap, well, once every 37 years—if they're lucky.

"Top to bottom, this is the best Tigers team I've ever seen since I've been in a Tigers uniform," declared Al Kaline, the Hall of Fame front office executive who has been a part of the organization for 55 years.

• • • •

It was all news to me. I didn't know anything about any trade in the works. I didn't know we were even talking to the Florida Marlins about Miguel Cabrera.

I had no sniff.

During the off-season, I basically become a fan until it's time to go to Florida again for spring training. For me, the off-season is a chance to play a little golf and spend more time with my wife, Lauri, and our four sons. During the season, obviously, I don't get to do that nearly as much as I would like.

So I was at home in St. Louis when a friend of mine, who has been a St. Louis Cardinals season-ticket holder since the 1960s, a guy who is a real baseball junkie, called me.

The first words out of his mouth were, "You guys just got better today."

I had no idea what he was talking about. I was completely out of the loop.

Certainly, nobody in the Tigers organization called to ask me what I thought about trading for Miguel Cabrera. Nobody asked me a thing. Nor would I expect them to. That's not the way it works in baseball. Guys like me are usually the last to know.

So right away, I said to my friend, "We did?"

I guess, to him, I must have sounded pretty clueless.

I had heard nothing about any trades involving the Tigers.

I go on the Internet a lot during the winter months. Of course, I always pay attention to what's going on with the Tigers and all throughout baseball. But nobody sniffed this one. Nobody was speculating about the Tigers trading for Miguel Cabrera. Nobody.

Anyway, my friend said to me, "You guys just got Miguel Cabrera."

I didn't believe him. I said, "Naw, you're kidding, right?"

We talked for a couple minutes, and when it finally sunk in that the trade really was happening, my first reaction was, "What a great addition for us!"

I only believed it could possibly be happening because I knew the value of Andrew Miller and Cameron Maybin.

It was the perfect relationship between the Florida organization's philosophy and the philosophy and new commitment in Detroit.

I knew we were willing to risk trading young talent in exchange for proven talent at the big-league level. We wanted to win.

But the Marlins' philosophy is, they're willing to get rid of proven value in exchange for young talent so that they don't have to spend as much in players' salaries and they can build for the future.

If someone in the organization had called me today and asked what I thought about the trade, my initial reaction would have been, "Great! Put Miguel Cabrera in left field, right field, center field. Heck, put him at catcher. Just put that bat in the lineup." That's just my opinion. I don't know what's going to happen. But I'll tell you this: I'm looking forward to spring training already.

JANUARY 12, 2008
DETROIT, MI

A sellout crowd of 8,500 showed up at chilly Comerica Park for FanFest this afternoon. They came out in the cold to get their first look at Miguel Cabrera and the rest of the mighty team that nearly everyone expects to muscle its way to the Central Division title and the American League pennant this summer.

"I don't see this many people for a game in Florida," joked Cabrera, as he eyed the long line of fans bundled up against the winter weather, patiently waiting for his autograph. "I can't wait to see Opening Day."

Neither can those fans, Miguel. Tickets for the 2008 season are already selling at a record rate.

Meanwhile, Jim Leyland, well aware of what people are saying about his loaded lineup, is already trying to hold expectations in check, insisting that the Cleveland Indians and the Boston Red Sox—not the Tigers—are the teams to beat in the AL this year.

The Tigers' manager cringes every time he hears the words *Murderers' Row*.

Leyland knows that the Tigers will be one of the chosen teams this spring— one of the teams the national reporters from *Sports Illustrated*, ESPN, CBS Sports, *USA Today*, and the other media outlets that tour the top training camps will make a point of visiting. Some more than once.

Leyland knows keeping his high-priced, high-powered team focused on the prize that awaits at the end of the season won't be easy.

.   .   .   .

Back in 2005 I was doing a little broadcasting as an analyst for the St. Louis Cardinals games, which I thoroughly enjoyed, by the way, and I was playing a little tournament golf on the Celebrity Tour. I was playing in some local events in the St. Louis area, too. After I retired as a player in 1995, I had done some work on the TV show *Best Damn Sports Show Period*. My life was pretty good, but I missed baseball. After all, the game had been a major part of my life from 1979 to 1995.

I had thought about coaching, but I wasn't sure that was something I wanted to do. I had thought about managing, too. I still would like to manage someday. I've thought about it a lot. I could go back to Single A ball and manage. But I don't know if I want to do that. That's the problem. The money, the travel—I don't know if I want to spend four or five years in the minor leagues doing that. You know, out of sight, out of mind.

Anyway, I happened to be in Pittsburgh for Mario Lemieux's golf tournament in June 2005, when I ran into Jim Leyland at a Pirates game at PNC Park one night. I had played for Jim in Pittsburgh from 1987 to 1994, and I had heard rumors that he might be getting back into managing again at the major-league level.

Jim was doing some scouting for the Cardinals at the time, and he walked into the stadium prepared, as any scout would be—with a pack of cigarettes.

Jim and I have always gotten along very well, so after we shook hands and visited for a few minutes, I said to him, sort of tongue-in-cheek, "Hey, if you're going to manage again and you need a coach, give me a call." I was really just sort of thinking out loud. I wasn't applying for a job or anything.

Jim said, "All right."

That was all there was to it. To tell you the truth, I put it completely out of my mind. I was only half-serious anyway. That was the last time I thought about it until Jim called me in September.

He said, "Are you serious about getting into coaching?"

The question caught me by surprise. I said, "Yeah, I'm serious," even though I wasn't sure I really was.

Then Jim said, "Well, be prepared. I'm not going to tell you where, but I might get back into managing again."

When Jim took the job with the Tigers after the 2005 season ended and they fired Alan Trammell, he called me again and said, "The job is yours, if you want it. But you gotta let me know one way or the other in a couple of days."

So that night I sat down at the dining room table at home with my whole family—my wife, Lauri, and our four sons, A.J., Scott, Jared, and Nathan. I remember my wife made spaghetti and meatballs for dinner that night.

I said, "All right. We're going to have a vote. This job is going to mean I'll be away from home more than half the year. So all of you who are in favor of me taking a job as a coach with the Detroit Tigers, raise your hands."

Five hands went up. My wife and our four kids all voted for me to take the job. I was the only one at the table who didn't raise his hand. I was outvoted. That was how I became the first-base coach of the Detroit Tigers.

Chapter 2

SPRING TRAINING

"I'm as Excited as Anyone"

FEBRUARY 11, 2008
LAKELAND, FL

I made my first trip to Lakeland, Florida—this once-sleepy small Central Florida city that has been the Tigers' spring-training home for 72 years—in 1970. But I have never sensed as much excitement, as much anticipation over the coming season, as I sense here this spring.

Tigers fans, without a World Series championship to celebrate since 1984, are understandably eager for the opportunity to root for a winner again. Like team owner Mike Ilitch and the Tigers players themselves, the fans, whose spirits are buoyed by the major off-season acquisitions and the resulting franchise-record $139 million payroll, are certain this will finally be their year.

Tickets for this spring's 17 exhibition games at cozy Joker Marchant Stadium, capacity 9,000 including standing room, have been selling at a record rate, just like those for the regular season at Comerica Park. The Tigers expect to attract more fans this spring than they did in the exhibition seasons following their 1968 and 1984 world championship seasons combined.

The first person I spotted this morning when I walked into the Marchant Stadium clubhouse for the first time this spring was Joel Zumaya, the injury-plagued, flame-throwing, tattooed rock-star right-handed reliever.

Zumaya, the heir apparent to Todd Jones' job as bullpen closer someday, underwent major reconstructive shoulder surgery last October 31. According to Zumaya, he was reaching up to remove some belongings from the attic in his family's home near San Diego, which was then threatened by wildfires, when a box filled with "between 50 and 60 pounds" of keepsakes from the Tigers' 2006 World Series came crashing down on his outstretched right shoulder.

Today, a thin red scar is all that remains of Zumaya's successful surgery. However, the mental scars left by the innuendoes and skepticism that raged across the Internet and on Detroit talk radio in the wake of his freak accident—nasty rumors that he fell off a motorcycle or that he hurt his shoulder falling off a couch while having sex—have not faded so quickly.

"It's tough having people who don't even know me or know what happened calling me a liar," Zumaya said this morning. "My family and friends hear people say things or they see things on the Internet, and they come to me and say, 'Hey, we heard this' or 'We heard that.' I don't know what I did to deserve this. It's sad, really.

"Last Friday some guy came up to me and said, 'Hey, you're not going to come into camp hurt again, are you?' Then he had the nerve to ask for my auto-graph."

Zumaya was so anxious to get to spring training so he could start proving his critics wrong that he loaded his kid brother Richard, a Tigers' farmhand, along

The promising career of relief pitcher Joel Zumaya, who possesses the best fastball in the American League according to *Baseball America*, continued to be star-crossed in 2008, as he was limited to 21 games because of two stints on the disabled list.

with their 65-year-old grandmother, Tammy, into Joel's four-door white GMC pickup, and drove from San Diego, California, to Lakeland, Florida—a distance of 2,100 miles—in just 34 hours.

"When I'm out on the open road, I fly," a smiling Zumaya admitted.

"Grandma got freaked out a couple of times, but she got used to it. She was telling me when I was clear. She'd say, 'You got it! Go! Go!'"

Not that Zumaya ever needed any encouragement to put the pedal to the metal—in anything.

. . . .

The thing that people forget is that there's a reason young players do things like Joel Zumaya does. He's a kid. He's really no different from any young kid we send to the front lines in wartime.

No kid ever thinks he's going to get shot running out of a foxhole. And Zumaya never thinks he's going to get hurt.

I heard about the rumors, too. But it's irrelevant what really happened to him this winter. To me, that doesn't matter. It doesn't matter if he got hurt moving boxes, like he said, or if he got hurt doing something else.

I've been there. We've all been there. We were all young once. You can't criticize Joel Zumaya for being young.

If he had been pitching for 10 years in the big leagues, he probably wouldn't have done something that hurt his arm. But he hasn't, and he did.

Losing him has a huge effect on our ballclub. There's no question about that; it hurts.

He and Fernando Rodney had as big an impact as any two guys on our ballclub in 2006 when we won the pennant and went to the World Series. The two of them were as important as Todd Jones, our closer, or any of our hitters.

Zumaya's injury will give an opportunity to some other pitchers in our bullpen. We'll see if they can do the job or not. We don't know that yet.

But with Zumaya out, we're going to find out.

FEBRUARY 15, 2008
LAKELAND, FL

This wasn't an easy winter for Brandon Inge. The popular, slick-fielding third baseman, who struggled at the plate last season—batting a disappointing .236—lost his job in December when the Tigers traded for Miguel Cabrera.

Some in the Tigers organization immediately began to think of Inge, who was the team's regular catcher from 2001 to 2003, as the logical replacement for Ivan Rodriguez when Pudge's contract expires at the end of this season.

But Inge isn't buying that. Inge, who lost his job behind the plate in 2004 when the Tigers signed the free agent Rodriguez, only to find a new home—and happiness—at third base, now feels like the odd man out again.

"Isn't this funny?" Inge said today as we walked from the Marchant Stadium clubhouse to the practice fields, across the old airport runway at Tigertown. "Everyone else walks out with the team, and I walk out with the media."

Inge knows this isn't likely to be an easy spring—or season—for him. He has told the Tigers he would like to be traded to a team where he can play third base every day. But so far nobody has knocked on Dave Dombrowski's door with such a deal.

Inge, for now a $19.1 million utility man, vowed not to become a cancer in the Tigers clubhouse.

"As much good stuff as we've got going on around here, nobody wants to hear about my crap," he said softly.

After practice today, in an effort to clear the air and set the record straight, Inge joined Jim Leyland for a little press conference in the manager's cramped Marchant Stadium office, with the larger-than-life photo of snarling Tigers icon Ty Cobb hanging on the wall.

"Do you want me to sit on your lap?" quipped Inge, ever the jokester, as he slid behind Leyland's desk.

"Here, do you want my chair?" the Tigers' gravel-throated manager responded, matching Inge's grin with one of his own.

"I don't want to lose Brandon Inge—but I hope I lose Brandon Inge so he can go someplace and play third base every day," declared Leyland, who called Inge "arguably the best defensive third baseman in the American League."

"If that doesn't happen, this is one manager who will be ecstatic to have Brandon Inge on his ballclub. I don't mind having Brandon Inge for as long as I can have him."

Leyland said the Tigers intend to "make every effort to trade Brandon," even though the manager admitted, "Without question, we'll be a weaker ballclub without Brandon Inge.

"We owe this man that respect," Leyland said.

For his part, Inge said, "The Detroit Tigers are in my blood. But there's not a starting role here for me, and I want to play every single day. For me, to sit on the bench crushes me. It kills me.

"When I moved to third base [in 2004], I thought I'd found a home. I was thinking I was going to be there for the rest of my career. Now I have to go back behind the plate. It's going to be tough.

"My first wish is to be traded," continued Inge, who is beginning his 10th spring training in Tigertown. "My heart is really at third base. I'd love to be a starting third baseman. But I'm not expecting anything. I'm a Detroit Tiger. And I have to assume I'll be a Detroit Tiger for the remainder of this contract [which runs through 2010]. I signed a four-year contract [in 2007] to play here, and I intend to fulfill that contract.

"I'm going to do anything I can to help this ballclub. I'm never going to be a cancer. I don't want this to be a distraction for the organization or for this team."

Inge said his personal situation came into perspective earlier this week while he, his wife Shani and their two kids were driving from their home in Greenville, South Carolina, to Lakeland, Florida.

"As I was driving, I was thinking about everything that was happening, and I was getting very angry," Inge admitted.

"We stopped at a gas station, and I was playing catch for a few minutes with my three-year-old son, Tyler, when another family pulled up, towing a U-Haul trailer. They got a wheelchair out of the trunk and lifted their little kid into it."

That was when Inge stopped feeling sorry for himself.

"Hey, I'm still able to put a big-league uniform on," he said.

There are worse things in life.

. . . .

Brandon Inge is an interesting situation. The Tigers did everything they could do this winter to accommodate his career. Believe me, we did.

A lot of times, players don't appreciate how far organizations go for them. The Tigers did everything they could.

Having said that, the Tigers were determined to make sure, in accommodating Inge's career, that they were also doing everything possible to make themselves better. They were not going to make themselves weaker just to accommodate Brandon Inge.

That's the business aspect of the game. Players are a commodity, just like everything else in the game.

Brandon Inge is a valuable part of this team coming into spring training. He is the most athletic baseball player I've seen in my 25 years in baseball. I've seen a lot of great athletes, but I've never seen an athlete, I can't even think of one, who could do what Brandon Inge can do.

Given six weeks to work at it, Brandon Inge could do just about anything in baseball except maybe be a starting pitcher. He could help a team in any other position on the field.

I have no doubt he could be a relief pitcher. Not just any relief pitcher, but a good enough reliever to pitch the seventh and eighth innings with the game on the line.

He can play third base, he can play shortstop, he can play second base or first. He can catch, he can play left field, center field, or right. And, like I said, he could be a seventh- or eighth-inning relief guy. And he could potentially win a Gold Glove at every position.

He's that good, athletically.

He could play all eight positions in the same game— and embarrass the regular starting players at every one of those positions. You can't say that about any other athlete in the history of the game. That's how athletic he is; that's how valuable he is. The Tigers know that; we understand his value.

We are very sensitive to what happened to Brandon Inge in the off-season when we traded for Miguel Cabrera.

But it was not a mistake to sign him to the contract for four years and $24 million. Inge hit 27 home runs in 2006 and drove in 83 runs. He just happened to have a bad year last year. He was doing some things at the plate that he probably shouldn't have been doing. But I think he has corrected that.

I still think that if Inge is given the chance this year, he'll match those numbers from 2006.

FEBRUARY 18, 2008
LAKELAND, FL

Miguel Cabrera—so big, so young, so rich, and so talented—made his much-awaited debut in the Marchant Stadium clubhouse this morning. As Cabrera walked around the room looking for his locker, he couldn't help but notice the nameplates mounted above the cubicles: Gary Sheffield, Magglio Ordonez, Carlos Guillen, Edgar Renteria, Pudge Rodriguez, Curtis Granderson, Placido Polanco. And Cabrera couldn't help but smile.

"It feels like my first day in the big leagues," said the Tigers' 24-year-old, 6'4", 240-pound slugger—down from a reported 260 pounds. "I'm excited."

That's exactly what the Tigers wanted to hear and see. "He's a man," Jim Leyland said, "a young superstar. When you were as horseshit a baseball player as I was, you know how hard it is to play this game—and you respect what guys like that can do. This guy has all the ingredients to be a total big-time player for a long time.

"When he steps in that batter's box, I don't care what he weighs," Leyland said. "Some guys are just big guys. They're big for a reason. I don't want to turn him into Twiggy.

"When you get a hitter as good as him, your job as a manager is to stay out of the way," Leyland admitted.

"Am I going to talk to Miguel Cabrera about hitting? Absolutely not one f*cking time! But," Leyland added, "when he goes to Cooperstown, I want people to say he was one helluva player—not just one helluva hitter."

Cabrera's first day in a Tigers uniform and already people are talking about the Hall of Fame.

. . . .

To tell you the truth, I wasn't really concerned about Miguel Cabrera today. I may have been the only one around Marchant Stadium who wasn't. But my job was to focus on my outfielders, to get them ready to play.

I let everybody else worry about Cabrera's presence and Edgar Renteria's presence and [19-year-old rookie pitcher] Rick Porcello's presence.

But I have to admit, when I first saw Cabrera, I was surprised at how big he is. His stature is bigger than I expected, and not in a negative way. I don't mean fat, because I know a lot of people have made a big deal about that with him. I'm talking about his physical presence. He looks bigger and stronger than I expected.

Living in St. Louis, I never heard about any weight issues with him. The few times I saw him play in St. Louis, from a distance, obviously I thought he was imposing. But when I saw him up close for the first time today, he was even more imposing than he appeared from a distance.

He's big everywhere. He's got a big head, he's got big feet, he's got big calves, he's got big hands. And I like his demeanor; he's very likable. He's just a big, likable kid. He wants to play. I think he wants to have fun.

If he does anything here in his next four years like he did in his first four years in Florida, there's no reason why the people in Detroit won't love him.

I sense that underneath that big, teddy-bear exterior, he likes to compete, too. He doesn't like to lose. He's like any bear: they look fuzzy and cuddly and cozy, but they'll bite your head off and eat you, too. I think that's how Cabrera competes.

This is a brand-new career for him. He's going from a young star who felt he had to prove himself in Florida, to a guy who is now in a role where he has to be able to carry this club. Nobody knows how that's going to work out. Nobody. Cabrera doesn't know, either.

That will be the most interesting thing. In the next two years, we'll find out whether or not he's going to be able to fulfill people's expectations of carrying the club, like a lot of Hall of Famers do when they're in their primes. You don't know.

I do think having Carlos Guillen and Magglio Ordonez alongside him in the locker room will help. Especially Guillen. Carlos is as smart and dedicated a player as I've ever been around. He knows the game. He and Cabrera are both from the same country—Venezuela. I think Carlos' veteran presence is going to have a huge influence on Cabrera's career.

MARCH 11, 2008
LAKELAND, FL

Major League Baseball, reacting to the death of minor-league coach Mike Coolbaugh—who was tragically killed last summer when he was struck by a batted ball while in the coach's box—has mandated that all first-base and third-base coaches must wear batting helmets this season.

The new policy has already given Tigers first base coach Andy Van Slyke a headache.

. . . .

This rule doesn't have the best interest of the people who wear the uniforms in mind. Those helmets are very hot, and they give me a headache every day. It's brutal to have to wear them for two and a half or three hours. I might put an ice bag under there to keep cool. I don't know what I'm going to do in Texas in that heat. It may cause somebody to overheat and have a heart attack.

I faced Randy Johnson in his first start in the big leagues, when he had no idea where the ball was going. He threw one pitch right under my chin. I could feel the wind off it. So I think I know how to get out of the way of a baseball.

Of all the things for Baseball to be worried about—I don't really understand it. Nobody has given me an explanation. No one has logically thought this thing through. If they're so worried about safety, they ought to make the pitchers wear helmets, too.

There wasn't a problem here to begin with, so why are they trying to create a solution to a problem that doesn't exist? It is totally a knee-jerk reaction to what was a tragic accident—one that, I have to say, wearing a helmet wouldn't have prevented to begin with.

Maybe they should just eliminate the first- and third-base coaches altogether, because there is no 100 percent way to prevent a coach from being hurt at either first or third base. What's to prevent a coach from being hit in the chest with a line drive that stops his heart?

The fact that we wear helmets, in my humble opinion, is eyewash, because the part of our heads that we are protecting is the hardest part anyway.

MARCH 23, 2008
LAKELAND, FL

Last year, in just his second full season in the major leagues, Curtis Granderson batted .302; hit 23 homers, 38 doubles, and 23 triples; and stole 26 bases. Only two players in baseball history—a long-forgotten fellow named Wildfire Schulte in 1911 and the Philadelphia Phillies' Jimmy Rollins last season—ever put up a package of numbers like that.

Today the Tigers arrived at the ballpark to learn that their star center fielder, who was struck on the right hand yesterday by a pitch in Clearwater, Florida, just two batters before the exhibition game against the Phillies was canceled by rain, suffered a broken finger and will be sidelined for at least three weeks.

"I have no idea what I'm doing, so don't ask me about Granderson," grumbled Jim Leyland when he arrived at the ballpark this Easter Sunday morning.

"I have no idea whatsoever what the lineup is going to look like. I have no clue."

And Opening Day is just a week away.

•   •   •   •

Magglio Ordonez was Magglio Ordonez last season, Carlos Guillen had a great year, and Placido Polanco hit .341. But in my opinion, Curtis Granderson was our MVP. He was the most energetic player on the team.

I hear people say, "Curtis Granderson hasn't come close to realizing his full potential yet," but I don't buy that. What kind of potential are we talking about here?

If Curtis Granderson merely repeats last year's performance every year for the next nine years, he'll be a surefire first-ballot Hall of Famer. Period! How much more potential do we want out of this kid?

Curtis did something last year that had only been done twice before in the history of the game. A guy named Willie Mays came close. And Mays only did that once in his career.

One of the biggest problems in today's games is the fact that there is so much hype. The expectations piled on players and teams are unfair. Two years ago Curtis Granderson wasn't even expected to be our every-day center fielder. Now we're expecting him to be even better than he was last year. Is that fair? In the matter of one calendar year, look what he has done. And people are saying he hasn't reached his potential yet? Are you kidding me?

If people want to make an analogy of our offense, our offense is a fine-tuned, turbo-charged Porsche engine that requires 93-or-higher octane fuel in order to run efficiently. Curtis Granderson is our higher-than-93-octane fuel.

This is not a knock on Edgar Renteria or whoever we put at the top of our lineup until Curtis comes back from his broken finger. But when you put Edgar Renteria in that leadoff spot, he's 87-octane. Now, all of a sudden, you're going to get a few knocks in the engine. The fuel is just not the same. Curtis Granderson is an igniter in a way that is totally different from any other player on our roster. That's just reality. Curtis was the fuel that pushed our engine last year.

Obviously, his getting injured hurts the team. I think it's a big hurt. People don't want to talk about it. Obviously there's nothing we can do. We can't get upset about it, and it's not an excuse.

But right now, we still don't know how our offense is going to fit together because it really hasn't been together all spring.

MARCH 25, 2008
LAKELAND, FL

The Tigers called a press conference this afternoon to herald the signing of Miguel Cabrera to a seven-year, $141 million contract extension on top of the $11.3 million deal for 2008 that he signed in January.

At 24 years of age, after just four full years in the big leagues, Cabrera is now guaranteed $152.3 million through 2015.

And, as Cabrera's agent Fern Cuza admitted today, if Miguel had elected to take the Tigers to salary arbitration next year and then tested the free-agent market after the 2009 season, he might have reaped an even more fantastic fortune, possibly collecting as much as $250 million, more than 152 times the entire payroll of the Tigers' world championship team.

At that price the Tigers, who parted with their two most promising minor leaguers—Cameron Maybin and Andrew Miller—last December in order to get Cabrera, would probably have had to bow out of the bidding. They would have ended up trading away the pride of their farm system for just two seasons of Miguel Cabrera. So the Tigers were understandably anxious—and delighted— to get this deal done, even though it represents the biggest financial commitment in franchise history.

When Cabrera weighed the fortune that awaited him on the open market as a 26-year-old free agent against the guaranteed cash the Tigers were offering—plus the chance to play on a contending team with Venezuelan countrymen Carlos Guillen and Magglio Ordonez—he chose the Olde English *D*.

"Miguel made the final decision," Cuza said. "Once he saw what he might get on the market and what they were offering here, he said, 'I want to be somewhere I'll be happy going to work every day.' To Miguel, it was more important to play somewhere he was comfortable than to go for the almighty last dollar."

Besides, Cabrera will only be 32 when his current contract with the Tigers expires—making him eligible for free agency and another huge contract then.

. . . .

When I see the money guys are getting today, I just shake my head.

It's incredible how much things have changed in baseball in a relatively short period of time.

I was the first-round draft pick of the St. Louis Cardinals in 1979. I was the sixth player picked. But my career didn't exactly get off to a roaring start. The day after I was drafted, my high school team was playing in the state championship game. On my last at-bat, I hit the ball as hard as I ever hit a ball in high school, right at the second baseman. The ball took one hop and hit the second baseman right in the forehead. It ricocheted off his head to the shortstop, who threw the ball to first. The shortstop rushed his throw—I could run pretty good—and it was a bad throw. The first baseman had to stretch for the ball, and he accidentally tripped me. I ended up breaking my wrist on the play—one day after I got drafted.

It was a bad break to the bone that rotates your thumb and your wrist. Some people have circulation on both sides of that bone, and some people only have circulation on one side. I'm one of those unfortunate people who only has blood flow on one side of the bone, so it took me about eight months to completely heal.

The Cardinals signed me anyway. They had offered me a $65,000 bonus the day they drafted me. After I broke my wrist, they lowered their offer to $50,000. I signed anyway, because I really wanted to play baseball. But I wasn't real happy with the Cardinals, starting off my career.

Today, as the sixth pick in the draft, I probably would have signed for $7 or $8 million, but back then the teams weren't throwing that kind of money around. The next year, Darryl Strawberry was the No. 1 pick, and he signed with the New York Mets for somewhere around $210,000. Draft picks just didn't get big money in those days.

Still, breaking my wrist was the best thing that ever happened to me. My arm was in a cast, and I ended up staying home that summer instead of going off somewhere to play minor-league ball. I spent that summer with a girl, Lauri, whom I ended up marrying. We just celebrated our 25th anniversary. If I had been off playing baseball in the minor leagues somewhere, we never would have hooked up.

It really was the best break I've ever had in my life, if you'll pardon the pun.

I grew up just outside Utica, New York, but I didn't like the Yankees. I was a Mets fan growing up, only because my friend, who lived across the street, was a fan of the Yankees. We had to have battles over everything, not only on the playground but also about which major-league teams we rooted for.

In February 1980 I went to spring training with the St. Louis Cardinals' minor leaguers, and I was eventually sent out to their farm team in Gastonia, North Carolina.

The socioeconomic atmosphere there was the complete opposite of what I had been exposed to, growing up in Utica. It was a racist area; the Ku Klux Klan had a chapter in Gastonia. I'd had a black girlfriend in high school, so you can image what a culture shock that was for me. Racism was something completely foreign to me. I kind of knew it existed, but I had never experienced it. So it was very eye-opening.

There I was, a 19-year-old kid, away from home for the first time, living in the South for the first time, in that atmosphere, experiencing a lot of things I had never experienced before in my life. Let's just say I started burning the candle at both ends—even though Gastonia was dry at the time. Freedom can be a dangerous thing. Where there's a will, there's a way—if you know what I mean.

I hit .330 the first half of the 1980 season, and I ended up hitting .270 for the year. So you can imagine what kind of second half I had. It all caught up with me.

In spring training of 1981 I tripped over the first baseman and broke my elbow. I missed the first couple months of the season and ended up hitting .220 with St. Petersburg in the Florida State League. I had a really bad year.

I played Double A ball in Arkansas in 1982, had a much better year, and went to Puerto Rico to play winter ball. That was really good for my career. In 1983 I was promoted to Triple A. I was hitting .368 at Louisville when I got called up to the Cardinals on June 15, 1983.

I was finally in the big leagues.

MARCH 27, 2008
LAKELAND, FL

The Tigers broke camp after today's game, a 14–5 pounding of the Phillies that Tigers fans can only hope is a harbinger of things to come. They'll fly to Houston tonight for two exhibition games against the Astros before returning home to open the season on Monday against Kansas City.

When spring training began seven weeks ago, Jim Leyland's three biggest tasks were finding a relief pitcher to temporarily replace Joel Zumaya, trading Brandon Inge, and settling on a batting order.

Today the Tigers departed Florida with Inge as their starting center fielder in place of the injured Curtis Granderson. Denny Bautista, Yorman Bazardo and Aquilino Lopez were in the bullpen, where everyone once assumed off-season acquisition Francisco Cruceta and holdover Fernando Rodney would be. New shortstop Edgar Renteria, who was supposed to bat seventh, will lead off, and Leyland is still undecided as to the identity of the 25th man on his squad.

"I like what I've seen the last few days," Leyland said, as he leaned back in his chair, put his stockinged feet up on his desk, and dug into a bowl of strawberry shortcake piled high with ice cream.

"The concentration level in our at-bats is picking up."

General manager Dave Dombrowski has done his part, trading for Miguel Cabrera, Edgar Renteria, Dontrelle Willis, and Jacque Jones. Owner Mike Ilitch has done his part, putting up the tens of millions needed to bring Pudge Rodriguez, Todd Jones, and Kenny Rogers back and to lock up Cabrera and Willis for the long term. Now the rest is up to Jim Leyland and the Tigers players. This weekend, in his final preseason address, Leyland intends to tell his team exactly that.

"We have no excuses, no cop-outs," the manager declared. "Nobody can say, 'They don't want to win here.' Not with this owner. This guy [Ilitch] has laid it out there. This guy has bent over backwards to make us good.

"It's conveniently and comfortably on the players now. We either do it or we don't."

. . . .

I'm as excited as anyone to see what this lineup can do. I had a hard time getting a sense of what the mood was like this spring because we've played so few games together as a lineup. We've never had our regular lineup in there for more than five innings at a time the whole spring. Of course, that's true most springs for most teams.

But it's hard for me to get a sense of what our lineup will look like when it's all together. I really don't know.

I know what these guys have done in the past. Everybody talks about this unbelievable offensive team. But that's strictly based on what guys have done in the past.

I'm as enthusiastic as anybody, but I've never been a hype guy. I've never gotten caught up in that. The only thing I really worry about is whether we have enough speed on our ballclub. I know how devastating a lack of speed can be.

Trust me, I'd rather have power hitters than speed guys any day. But I think it makes you that much better if you have some speed, too, to support that power. Speed never goes in to slumps. Never has, never will.

I think Curtis Granderson will ignite things for us once his hand heals and he comes back. But other than Curtis, we don't have much speed. We'll see what happens.

Chapter 3

APRIL

"Someone, Please Rescue Us"

MARCH 31, 2008
DETROIT, MI

As always, Comerica Park, which opened in 2000 to replace venerable but woefully outdated Tiger Stadium—located less than a mile away—was packed this afternoon for Opening Day, which has long been just short of a legal holiday in Detroit.

If the record advance-ticket sales are any barometer, a sold-out Comerica Park is going to be a frequent occurrence this season. The Tigers have already sold more than 30,000 tickets for most of their 81 home dates and are more than 850,000 ahead of last year's pace, when they attracted a franchise record 3,047,139 fans.

"Hooray for Mr. Ilitch, that's what I say," exclaimed Jim Leyland, who obviously knows where his bread is buttered.

A crowd of 44,934 showed up today to get a first glimpse of the Tigers' All-Star-studded juggernaut lineup. But they didn't get the outcome that everyone hoped for and expected.

Fans ended up pointing fingers at the jury-rigged bullpen as newcomer Denny Bautista, who this spring won the spot vacated by the injured Joel Zumaya and Fernando Rodney, took the loss, 5–4, for yielding a run on two hits to the Kansas City Royals in the top half of the 11th inning.

"The story line has been set," grumbled closer Todd Jones after the Tigers squandered 10 hits, including home runs by Miguel Cabrera and Carlos Guillen, plus five innings of one-hit pitching by Justin Verlander.

"That's just the way it's going to be this year," predicted Jones, who did his part in the game with a 1-2-3 ninth. "Everybody waits until the lead gets away late in the game, and then they say, 'See, I told you so.' Everybody says, 'There goes the ballgame again.' It's going to be a self-fulfilling prophecy.

"Everybody wants to take shots at us, to make fun of us," Jones complained, speaking out in defense of the entire relief corps. "Everybody is going to see what they want to see. It ticks me off. I take it personally when guys want to take shots at us.

"Everybody knows what our lineup is and who the starting pitchers are. Any bullpen is going to be looked at as a red-headed stepchild in that situation.

"This is probably the greatest lineup this town has seen in the last 25 years," Jones declared. "In this lineup, even Mr. [Al] Kaline would have to hit sixth or seventh.

"Of course," Jones added, "he's 70 years old."

Actually, Todd, Al Kaline is 73.

"This will be a tremendous year for fans, from a second-guessing stand-point," Jim Leyland predicted. "There'll be a lot of talk. I'm prepared for that. I think it'll be a fun year for people."

• • • •

I got 10 million phone calls for tickets for Opening Day this year—more than I've ever had before in my life. And I'm not even from Michigan. I never played here, either. It was amazing.

Actually, even though we lost 5–4 in the eleventh inning, it was a great game. This game had everything you want from a baseball game. It was as good as any Opening Day that I have ever been a part of.

Even though we got beat, we had good pitching, we had good defense, and we had timely hitting. That's all you can ask for. It was very competitive. We probably had an opportunity to score more runs, but, in fairness, so did the Royals.

We came from behind, we threw a guy out at home plate—like I said, this game had everything you want in a baseball game. Except a win, of course.

Otherwise, this was as good as an Opening Day game can get.

APRIL 8, 2008
BOSTON, MA

By the time Jim Leyland got to Fenway Park this morning, he was smiling, telling stories, and cracking wise, as usual. The gloom of the Tigers' shocking season-opening six-game losing streak against the Royals and Chicago White Sox had been set aside.

Then the game began. It was Opening Day in Boston. But for the Tigers, it was the same old story.

A year ago, without Miguel Cabrera and Edgar Renteria, the Tigers were only shut out three times all season. Today, after watching the Red Sox receive their World Series rings, the supposedly high-octane Tigers were blanked, 5–0.

It was, incredibly, their seventh loss in a row this young season—and their second shutout in their first seven games.

"We can keep talking about how good we are," said Kenny Rogers, today's losing pitcher. "But right now, we're the worst team in baseball."

The season is barely a week old and already the Tigers are five games out of first place. They didn't fall five games behind the division leader last year until August 31.

"Sometimes you can smell stuff," Leyland said. "And righ now we don't smell good. We've looked like a dead club. We've looked like an old club."

Of course, time is on the Tigers' side. They still have 155 games to play. But history is not on their side. No team that started a season 0–7 has ever recovered to advance to the postseason.

"I don't give a damn about what's happened in the last 100 years!" Leyland barked after the game. "I care about what's happening now."

.   .   .   .

This is the strangest beginning to a season that I've ever seen, without question.

Guys are starting to swing at a lot of bad pitches. When athletes start doing things that they don't normally do, it's a sign of mental panic.

Unless you've played this game, you don't understand that.

No general manager, no writer, no fan, no coach or manager who has never played the game can really understand that sense of panic that you feel.

It's panic in the sense that you're thinking, *I have to be* the guy *who does it. And I have to it right now,* right now...*or else.*

It's not something you say. It's something that is in your head.

You know it's not the right feeling to have. But you can't stop it.

It's like when someone starts to drown. The worst thing he can do is to start thrashing. The conversations on the bench have stopped being normal. There is a feeling like, "We're drowning. What are we going to do about it?"

Today the feeling in the dugout was, "Someone, please rescue us."

I don't know what the answer is going to be. Nobody does. Jim Leyland doesn't know; the players don't know.

When I watch documentaries on TV about war, I see soldiers who are shell-shocked. Today, in the clubhouse after the game, there was a sense of being shell-shocked. There was a real sense of being in a foxhole with a bunch of shells going off all around us. We're scared, we're stuck in a foxhole, and we're just waiting for the shelling to stop.

Guys are thinking, *This can't be happening. Not to us.* There is a sense that the next game might kill us, and that isn't the way this season was supposed to unfold.

As a coach, you don't know what to say to the players. Do you go up to them and say, "Are you okay?" Well, when you're hitting .086, you're not okay. You can't be disingenuous in this game. Believe me, that won't work. Especially not with veteran players like we have.

It's not like they're not trying. In some cases they're trying too hard. It's not like guys aren't enthusiastic. It's not quiet in the dugout or negative. The guys are all positive; they're cheering for one another.

But you can almost feel them thinking, *We've got to be positive. We've got to cheer because, if we don't, it will look like we're not trying.*

These guys really do show up to play every day. But we don't always play smart or play right or play the way we want to play. You can sense it in the dugout. Guys are thinking, *Let's do this...now!*

If we're playing .500 baseball by the end of the month, I think everything will be fine. If we're playing .500 baseball by the end of the month, we'll only be one or two games back, because nobody is going to run away with this thing.

No need to panic. There's still plenty of time.

APRIL 9, 2008
BOSTON, MA

The Tigers finally got off the *schneid* tonight, drubbing the world-champion Red Sox 7–2 for their first victory of the season, ending the fifth-worst start in the franchise's 108-year history.

"We're not out of the woods by any means," Jim Leyland admitted after the welcome win. "But I think this will loosen everybody up a little bit.

"I'm going to stay positive. But there is a difference between staying positive and being phony about it.

"I'm not the Lone Ranger. If we don't hit, I'm going to be with every other person in baseball, because everyone in baseball thinks this club is going to hit."

In the lobby of the Sheraton Boston Hotel before leaving for nearby Fenway Park this afternoon, Magglio Ordonez asked me, "What is the most losses a team has ever had at the start of the season?"

"The Tigers' record is 13 losses in a row," I told him.

Magglio frowned.

"Did they win that year?" Ordonez wanted to know.

"No, they did not," I said.

Magglio shook his head.

"Baseball is a very hard game to play," he replied.

Before tonight's game, Kenny Rogers punished himself for yesterday's defeat by staging a personal two-hour Boston Marathon during batting practice, running—or, more accurately, jogging—around and around Fenway Park, by his own count some 60 times, covering 12 to 13 miles.

"More than I probably should have," the exhausted, perspiring 43-year-old Rogers confessed later with a sheepish grin.

"He's crazy," first baseman Carlos Guillen said.

Ballplayers often run laps around the field or run up and down the stairs at empty ballparks before the gates open and the fans come in. But I dare say, in the history of the game, no 43-year-old pitcher has ever run the way Rogers did today.

Kenny isn't scheduled to pitch again until Sunday afternoon in Chicago. By then, he should have caught his breath.

. . . .

I have never been part of a major-league team that had a harder time getting a win. It's really been shocking. I've been on some bad teams that lost a lot of games. But this is a good team; this club was expected to win. Sometimes that makes it even harder to get things turned around.

In the fourth inning today, Edgar Renteria hit a two-run double, Marcus Thames hit a home run, and we finally got the lead. What's a lead? I don't know. We've had so few of them this year.

The players weren't exuberant in the clubhouse after the win. People weren't popping champagne, and they shouldn't be.

We've had the bases loaded a lot of times, but we've hit into a lot of double plays. Those are things that didn't happen around here during the last two years.

We knew we were going to be able to score runs against Boston. We weren't really too concerned. We just didn't want to fall too far behind. When you get way behind, it's hard to come back, especially against good teams like the Red Sox.

Everybody keeps waiting and waiting to see the real Tigers show up. We keep waiting for our time to come, too, and it hasn't come yet.

We still have egg on our faces, and we all know that. It's not like one win is going to change the reality of the situation.

We really need to get to .500. Until this club gets to .500, there should be no celebrating.

APRIL 13, 2008
CHICAGO, IL

Everyone knew an explosion was coming. It was merely a matter of when.

Just this morning, before the game, Jim Leyland was telling reporters how, as he lay in bed at his downtown Chicago hotel last night, wondering what he could do to turn this season around before it was too late, he ruled out another tirade like the one that so famously seemed to right the ship after the Tigers had mailed in a getaway day game against Cleveland back in April 2006. Although Leyland declined to claim any credit, that outburst turned the team and its season around.

But this is a different team and a different season and a different situation. At this point, Leyland told himself last night, screaming at his floundering players was not the proper thing to do. It wouldn't work.

However, after watching the Tigers waltz their way through a lackluster 11–0 loss to the Chicago White Sox in yet another getaway day game—their second whitewash in two days and their fourth shutout in their first 12 games—Leyland simply couldn't hold his emotions in check any longer.

Waiting in the corridor outside the door to the visiting team's clubhouse at U.S. Cellular Field, I couldn't help but hear the barrage of F-bombs, aimed at the Tigers players, exploding a few feet away inside the locker room.

If there is one thing Leyland will not tolerate, it is players going through the motions, wasting their at-bats.

Today, in the sixth, seventh, and eighth innings, after the Tigers had fallen behind 11–0 to the White Sox, it took the Chicago pitchers just 24 tosses to get the required nine outs.

Afterward Leyland refused to reveal exactly what set him off. But those of us who follow the Tigers on a daily basis believe that the players' feeble, half-hearted efforts on this bitterly cold April afternoon were what Leyland later called, "the straw the broke the camel's back for me."

Leyland ended his diatribe by screaming at his players, "Now get the f*ck out of here!"

Duly chastised, the defeated Tigers quickly showered and dressed—in proper silence, of course—then hurried out to board the chartered bus that would take them to the airport, where the team's private plane presumably waited to fly them home.

No one, including Leyland, knew at the time that the Tigers' plane, which also services the Mike Ilitch–owned Detroit Red Wings, was still on its way back from Nashville, where it had taken the hockey team, and would arrive in Chicago to pick up the Tigers some 90 minutes later than originally scheduled.

So, adding insult to injury, the 2–10 Tigers were told to get off the bus and go back and wait in the clubhouse—the very clubhouse where they had just been blistered by their irate manager.

In April 2006, after the Tigers put forth a similarly listless effort against the Indians, Leyland unleashed a similar outburst. Awakened, the Tigers, who had not enjoyed a winning summer since 1993 or a trip to the postseason since 1987, went on to win the American League pennant and advance to the World Series.

We shall see if it works again.

.   .   .   .

Let's get one thing straight right now: we don't like the Chicago White Sox. If there is one team that we really like to beat, it's not the Yankees, it's not the Red Sox, it's the White Sox. I think everybody in the American League likes to beat the White Sox. For many reasons.

What Jim Leyland expressed after the game, everybody felt. What he said needed to be said, and it came from the right person.

A lot of managers want to say things to their teams, but they end up saying things that deflect the responsibility away from themselves or away from the players. Some managers don't know what to say or how to say it to make guys look at themselves rather than look somewhere else, like at one of their teammates, or at a coach, or at the manager.

I played for Jim, I've coached under Jim, and he really has the unique ability to make everybody in the clubhouse look nowhere else but into the mirror at themselves.

But will it make a difference? Who knows?

APRIL 14, 2008
DETROIT, MI

The slumbering volcano that Tigers fans had been waiting all month to see finally erupted tonight, spewing 16 hits in a wild, 11–9, come-from-behind triumph over the Minnesota Twins.

The 32,002 well-chilled fans, many draped in blankets, who had been booing the disappointing last-place hometown team a few innings earlier, were all on their feet at the end, chanting and clapping and cheering for the Tigers' first win of the season at Comerica Park.

"I think this game said a lot about this team," said Jim Leyland, who a day earlier in Chicago had berated his players. "They could have packed it in. But I didn't see anybody packing it in.

"People ask me about our chemistry. When you're 2–10, that's horseshit chemistry. Show me a winning team, and I'll show you good chemistry."

·   ·   ·   ·

I have always believed that when you win a championship or you win your division, you can look back on certain games throughout the season that propelled you in the right direction. This is one of those opportunities that could propel us.

I'm not saying that's going to happen, but it certainly could be a cornerstone. A couple more games like this, and I think we're going to see our offense do what it is capable of doing.

The hardest part of this game, the thing that people don't understand, is that when you are struggling, players try to take on too much. They try to do it all on one particular pitch, or in one particular at-bat. And we've certainly been guilty of that.

That can be a good thing, and that can be a bad thing. You want guys to try to do as much as they can. But sometimes they extend too far.

Everybody in our lineup is capable of hitting two-run triples like Pudge Rodriguez did tonight. Everyone has that capacity. The hard part is doing it when you *have* to do it.

I thought the second inning of this game was another microcosm of our season.

We've got a Gold Glove Hall of Fame catcher in Pudge Rodriguez, whom I've never seen come close to dropping a pop-up—and he dropped one. I didn't even see him drop it. I was so sure he was going to catch it, I turned away to get ready for the next pitch. Then I heard the crowd's reaction, the groan, and I thought, *Oh, my gosh.*

Right away I got this sick feeling in my stomach because I knew the Twins were going to take advantage of it. When you give a big-league team an extra opportunity, they're usually going to score on you, especially good teams. And the Twins are a good team. And they did exactly that. They took a 2–0 lead in the second inning.

Then in the bottom half of the inning, when we got two guys on base and didn't click, I thought, *Gosh darn, this is a reflection of how our season is going.*

When we got down 5–0 in the sixth inning, there was a sickening feeling in my mind and, I think, in everybody's minds throughout the whole dugout.

When we got back into the game at 5–4, I really thought—and I think everybody thought—*We're going to win the game.*

That's how quickly your emotions can change during the course of a game, especially when you've been struggling the way we have.

Then we gave up four more runs in the seventh inning and all of a sudden we were down 9–4. I thought, *Man, this is going to be the hardest loss of the season.* And it really would have been. There is no question about that.

But what we thought was going to be the best part of our team finally showed up in the bottom of the eighth when we scored six runs to win the game.

With our ballclub, we're probably going to have to do an awful lot of that this season—coming from behind and scoring a whole lot of runs. We're going to need big innings, and today, we finally got a couple.

APRIL 16, 2008
CLEVELAND, OH

After scoring just 33 runs in their first 12 games, the Tigers have now put 30 runs on the scoreboard in their last three—all of them wins, two over the Minnesota Twins and one over the Cleveland Indians.

When an unknown minor leaguer named Armando Galarraga, just up from Toledo, outpitches Cy Young Award winner C.C. Sabathia, and you beat the team everybody said you had to beat in order to dominate the American League Central, 13–2, you have to assume you might be on a roll.

.   .   .   .

Armando Galarraga wasn't even in the equation back in spring training. And C.C. Sabathia was coming off a couple of bad starts. So before the game, we're thinking, *Well, C.C. is going to figure it out sooner or later*. We were just hoping tonight wasn't the night.

But Sabathia's pattern continued. He struggled in the strike zone. Even when he makes mistakes in the strike zone, he's still a good pitcher. His stuff is usually good enough to get away with it, but tonight he didn't get away with it. I think that was more of a reflection on our offense than on his bad pitching.

Tonight we stayed in the strike zone very well, we didn't swing at a lot of pitches outside the zone, and we also took our walks. That is an indication of a powerful offense.

Look at what the Yankees and the Red Sox have done over the last few years. They work the count with the pitchers. They get walks. Then, when they do get a good pitch to hit, they jump on it. We need to be that same type of offense.

Our offense for the first two weeks of the season was really a reflection of our overanxiousness more than anything else. I don't care how good an offense you have, you still have to swing at strikes in order to be successful in the big leagues. And for the first two weeks of the season, we were swinging at more pitches outside the strike zone than I had seen our team do in the past two years.

We were going outside the strike zone, trying to do too much at the plate in each at-bat. Everybody was doing that. Each guy was guilty of it. It wasn't any one particular hitter; guys were all expanding their strike zones.

Hopefully what happened during those first 14 games will help everybody remember what not to do. Because that philosophy of expanding the strike zone is not going to work—not if we're going to be successful.

APRIL 21, 2008
TORONTO, ON, CANADA

Jim Leyland's patience is wearing thin. Before today's game, a 5–1 matinee win over the Blue Jays in Toronto, he sent another profanity-laced message to his so-often-underachieving team.

"We've got a lot of talent here—but right now we don't have a lot of team," the frustrated manager told the press in his strongest public indictment yet of his struggling team, now 7–13.

"I take that personally," Leyland said. "I'm at the head of the class. I'm responsible for the performance of this team. And what's going on ain't f*cking good enough.

"They're better than this. I'm not rubbing their tummies right or something. I've got to do a better job of getting them ready. Everybody who pitches against us ain't f*ckin' Cy Young.

"There'll be no excuses here," Leyland continued. "All that bullshit is bullshit. This is the f*ckin' big leagues. I'm not going to make excuses for the players. That was the shit that went on before I got here.

"I've got to do better. The coaches have got to do better. And the players have got to do better. The big boys have got to step it up. We all need to step it up.

"They can be pissed off at me all they want. I'm tired of this. I'm tired of all the excuses. I want to see some f*ckin' action."

.   .   .   .

I pay a lot of attention to the things Jim Leyland does and the way he handles his team.

I played for Whitey Herzog in St. Louis and for Jim in Pittsburgh, and I've learned a lot from both of them. But they handle things differently.

The first thing I learned from Jim was that, not only is he intense as a manager, but he expects that intensity and that mental preparation from his players on a daily basis.

That wasn't the case when I was in St. Louis. With the Cardinals, I spent a lot of time sitting on the bench, pissed off because I wasn't playing. And that affects your performance on the field when you do get into the game. Jim never let that happen.

When Jim cut the strings from me and let me play every day in Pittsburgh, I had to learn how to prepare mentally every day. Jim really challenged me, almost on a daily basis. He was really good about that. He really helped my career and made me a better player because he raised the bar—not so much physically as mentally. Nothing happens physically until you're ready mentally. I don't want to say I was a passive player, but Jim really taught me how to play at a higher mental level.

The great thing about Jim was, you always knew where you stood with him. He was always honest with you. If Jim had something on his mind, he would come and tell you. If he had something to say to me, he said it to my face. I always appreciated that.

Whitey Herzog was a great strategist, but he always communicated through the media or through one of his coaches. And, in a lot of ways, that wasn't always positive. For some reason Whitey didn't see me as an every-day player. I saw myself as an every-day player—but Whitey didn't. I think that really stunted my growth as a major leaguer.

In a lot of ways, I was a victim of my own talent. I could play first base and third and all three outfield positions, so Whitey moved me around a lot. I got a lot of at-bats that way, but I think if I had been a guy who could play just one outfield position, I might have been better off.

I really think if Whitey had just stuck me out there and let me play every day, I would have become a better player. But that's ancient history now. I've got no complaints.

Today, rookie Armando Galarraga won another ballgame for us. To tell you the truth, the kid's winning doesn't make sense. But it doesn't make sense that we were 0–7 at the start of the season, either.

Come August and September, I think we're going to look back at this season and we're going to look back on particular games and particular series that kept us in the race. And I think Galarraga's first two starts in the major leagues, his first two wins, may be something we look back on.

We're not in full gear yet. It was a bad feeling when we lost those two games to the Blue Jays on Saturday and

Sunday. We thought we had crawled out of what we were doing poorly, and then we slipped right back into it for a couple days.

But I still believe we have only lost one well-played game this year, and that was Opening Day. That game, we did everything right and still lost. We haven't done everything right and had another loss since then.

I think that's a good sign. For us to be competitive and get back into this race and hopefully end up in first place, we're going to have to do everything right.

APRIL 22, 2008
DETROIT, MI

Tonight's 10–2 victory over the Texas Rangers was barely finished when Jim Leyland interrupted his postgame press conference at Comerica Park to drop a bombshell: Effective immediately, Miguel Cabrera, the Tigers' $152.3-million third baseman, will be moving to first base, and former-shortstop-turned–first baseman Carlos Guillen will be shifting to third. Obviously Cabrera's defense at third, which had Tigers fans concerned, worried Leyland, too.

The young slugger, who belted his fourth home run tonight, has made five errors, all at third base. Meanwhile, he has looked increasingly comfortable in the three games where he has filled in at first base.

"We think, at this point, this makes us a better team—period," declared Leyland, who declined to elaborate or explain his decision.

"There are no questions to answer," he said. "We're doing this because we think it gives us our best chance to win."

"It's cool," Cabrera said.

"Everybody's happy," said Guillen, the team's shortstop last season who volunteered to move to first base this year, paving the way for the Edgar Renteria trade.

In a move to bolster the Tigers' shaky defense, third baseman Miguel Cabrera (right) and first baseman Carlos Guillen swapped positions on April 22. "We think, at this point, this makes us a better team—period," declared manager Jim Leyland. *Photo courtesy of AP Images.*

Meanwhile, Brandon Inge, who lost his job at third base when the Tigers acquired Cabrera, remains a player without a position.

· · · ·

It doesn't come down to who is a better first baseman or who is a better third baseman. It gets down to what makes our team better right now. And I think, at this point, this move makes us better.

It's not that one guy is being demoted and one guy is being promoted. It's a matter of utilizing the talent we have where it is most advantageous to our team. Both Carlos and Miguel are still going to hit like they always have. I'm talking about defense here. It's like moving a middle linebacker to outside linebacker in football.

Miguel Cabrera is a big, talented person. He's got soft hands, and he'll learn. There is some footwork involved at first base, but there was footwork involved at third base, too.

I think the big thing is that, off the ball, Carlos is quicker than Miguel. That's a fact. And third base requires quickness.

I think, in the long run, they'll both see how beneficial this change is to the ballclub.

APRIL 29, 2008
NEW YORK, NY

With Curtis Granderson back in the lineup and leading off, the Tigers topped the New York Yankees, 6–4.

In the 21 games while Granderson was sidelined with a broken bone in his right hand, his replacements in the lead-off position scored a total of just three runs. In Curtis' first six games back, he has scored 11 times, including three runs tonight.

• • • •

During the off-season, people always wanted to talk to me about the individual accomplishments on our ballclub last year, such as Magglio Ordonez hitting .363 and winning the batting title, Placido Polanco winning his Gold Glove and his errorless streak and his 200 hits, Curtis Granderson with his 20–20–20–20 year, and Carlos Guillen being an All-Star.

When you looked at the individual accomplishments of last year, then added Miguel Cabrera, Edgar Renteria, and Jacque Jones, everybody thought we were going to have a solid offense this season.

But like I told everybody, the reason we have a good offense is because we have the best lead-off hitter in the game. I don't think it's any accident that, since Curtis has been back, the offense has taken on a whole different personality. It's totally different.

When you have a guy who has the physical ability to put fear in the pitcher, whether that pitcher walks him or throws him a 3–1 fastball, you have a very unique baseball player. There're not many players in the game who can cause a pitcher to dread walking them and dread throwing them a 3–1 fastball at the same time. That's what makes Curtis Granderson a complete player. We're going to go as Curtis Granderson goes. He is *the guy*.

As I said before, it's sort of like owning a Porsche. I know because I used to own one. You're supposed to put in gas that is 93 octane or higher. Our offense without Curtis

Granderson was like putting regular gas into a Porsche. It performs, but it doesn't perform at its peak. Curtis Granderson is our 93 octane.

It's no accident that since Granderson came back, Placido Polanco, who bats right behind him, has started hitting. When those two guys do what they're capable of doing, you're going to see everyone else follow suit.

A lot of times players put self-imposed pressure on themselves. They're trying to hit three-run homers with nobody on base because they feel they've got to do it right then and there all by themselves. Of course, nobody can do that.

When Granderson and Polanco are hitting at the top of our lineup, the other players feel they don't have to do it all by themselves. Then they know a single will score a run.

It really dissipates that pressure.

APRIL 30, 2008
NEW YORK, NY

The Tigers hit three more home runs tonight in their 6–2 win over the Yankees. That makes 17 home runs in their last nine games. They are now 13–2 when scoring five or more runs. It's obvious what they need to do.

The Tigers, who have won seven out of their last nine games, finished April with a 13–15 record—the first time they have posted a losing record during the first month of the season since 2003, when they were 3–21. But, after starting the year 0–7 and then 2–10, nobody is complaining.

·　·　·　·

I rode the subway out to Yankee Stadium for tonight's game. I do that a lot when we play in New York. It's a lot cheaper than taking a cab, it's usually quicker than a cab, and the people you see on the subway are a real trip.

I love New York—the nightlife, energy, cynicism, and skepticism that exists in this city. It's such a unique place. I think it's a tremendous cultural experience. Would I choose to live here? Probably not. But if I had a real good reason to move to New York, I wouldn't have a problem with it, at least not at this point in my life. I wouldn't want to raise kids in the city, but my kids are grown.

Having said that, I was glad to see today that they finally took the *Wanted* poster of me down off the wall in the subway station after what happened here last year. My wife didn't think so, but that little incident last year was the most fun I've ever had in New York.

It was after a day game and my wife, my sister-in-law, her daughter, and I were going right from Yankee Stadium to a restaurant where we were going to meet my brother-in-law for dinner. I paid for four fares, and you're supposed to be able to swipe the ticket at the turnstile four times to let four people through.

Well, it let my sister-in-law and her daughter go through all right. But when it came time for my wife and I to go through the turnstiles, the ticket wouldn't work anymore. I had put eight bucks into the machine, but for some reason it only gave us credit for two $2 fares.

So my wife and I were standing there swiping the card over and over, my sister-in-law and her daughter were waiting for us on the other side of the turnstile, and the people coming out of the ballpark were piling up behind us.

They were mad and were yelling, "Come on, let's go! What's the holdup?"

So I said to my wife, "Let's just jump over this thing."

I pushed her under the turnstile and I jumped over it. Well, we didn't take three steps before a cop grabbed me and another cop grabbed my wife. They put us both up against the wall right there in the subway station. The funny thing was, it was a female cop who grabbed me and a male cop who grabbed my wife. They both looked like they were just out of the police academy.

Anyway, they had us up against the wall, and my wife, Lauri, was so embarrassed. Then some of the fans who were leaving the game recognized me and started yelling, "Hey, Andy! How ya doin'!" And some of them were chanting, "Jumper! Jumper! Van Slyke's a jumper!"

The two cops were both looking back over their shoulders wondering, *Who are these two people we just stood up against the wall?*

While the cop was writing my ticket, one guy came up to me and said, "Hey, Andy. Can I have your autograph?" The cop shooed him away.

My wife looked over at me and said, "I hate you right now."

I said, "You know, I love it when you're angry at me." Honestly, I thought it was hilarious.

I had stuck both hands in my pockets, and the female cop said, "Take your hands out of your pockets."

I said, "I'm not carrying a gun, but I am packing." I thought that might have been my best line of the year.

At that point my wife was really humiliated. She put her hands over her face and said, "You can't embarrass me any more than you are right now."

To me, that was the funniest part of the whole thing: embarrassing my wife.

Once the cops finished writing the tickets, they let us go. They figured they were way ahead of the game by then.

The tickets were $150 apiece, so my wife and I paid $300 for a $4 subway ride. Actually, we paid $304 because I had already paid our fares. The city came out way ahead on that deal.

Of course, the adventure wasn't over. After all that, in the confusion, we ended up getting on the wrong train. If you've ever ridden the subway in New York, you know what an adventure that can be. I finally realized we were going the wrong way, and I said, "Let's just get off the train and grab a cab."

When we finally got to the restaurant, my brother-in-law, who was already there with some other people, said, "Where have you been? We've been here for 45 minutes?"

Chapter 4

MAY

"Our Offense Doesn't Make Sense"

MAY 4, 2008
MINNEAPOLIS, MN
After three wins in New York, the Tigers arrived in Minnesota on Friday riding high and finally feeling good about themselves. They left town late this afternoon with their tails tucked between their legs after losing three in a row to the perennially pesky Twins, including today's 7–6 beating in which they inexcusably blew a six-run first-inning lead.

Too many lazy fly balls off the bats of Tigers batters, too many easy infield pop-ups, too many futile trips to the plate, and too many mediocre pitchers made to look like Hall of Famers by the Tigers' so-called Murderers' Row lineup left Jim Leyland vowing to "shake things up" tomorrow when the team returns home to open a seven-game homestand against the world champion Red Sox and the revenge-minded Yankees.

"I'm shocked," Leyland admitted after the latest loss. "For whatever reason, and I don't know why, we haven't had the sense of urgency that we need. It's almost like we think, *We've won a couple of games, so now it's okay to lose a couple*. We just haven't had that kick in the ass to get us over the hump.

"Right now we're 3F— fouled up, fed up, and far away from here."

·　·　·　·

Our offense, at times, just does not make sense.

Coming out of New York after that sweep, I thought maybe we had finally stopped grinding our gears. I thought we were ready to roll. But the first day in Minnesota, we laid an egg. And the second day here, we laid another egg. It's no more complicated than that.

The first two games against the Twins, nothing happened with our offense. Minnesota outscored us 15–2 in those two games. That just shouldn't happen.

Today we got a six-run lead in the first inning and Murphy's Law was right out there in front of the Twins. Everything that could go wrong for them did go wrong in that first inning.

They made an error, and we had two bloop hits that you'll never see the rest of the year. Sure, we got five hits in a row. But there it was, 6–0, and I was thinking to myself, *How did that happen?*

Okay, we were up 6–0 in the first inning, and that's something we hadn't seen yet this season. We're usually pretty good at adding on runs in the middle of the game, but today that didn't happen. And all of sudden Murphy's Law was turned around in our faces.

Carlos Guillen made an error at third base on a play that he makes 99 times out of 100. That error just killed us, and Carlos knows it.

In the big leagues, when you give a team an extra out at home, it's amazing how many times you lose the game because of it. It doesn't matter who you're playing against or who makes the error. That's just the reality of the game, especially in Minnesota in the Metrodome.

Then they got a blooper and they got a chopper up the middle, and the game was over. It was amazing.

Going home 4–2 would have looked a whole lot better than 3–3, especially after the way we started off this road trip in New York.

I don't think there was a letdown in Minnesota. I don't think there was a letdown at all. I don't think the team has had any letdowns all year.

We've got a lot of good players on this team right now, and we're going to have a lot of good players on this team in September. We're good, but I don't know if we really believe that yet.

The question is: are we going to be a good team or not? I don't know the answer to that yet. I don't think anybody in this clubhouse knows. I don't think anybody knows if they're going to be a good team or not—until they are.

The mentality of a professional baseball team is amazing. Whatever you think, whatever you believe, whether it is right or wrong, that is what is true. Whether you think you can or whether you think you can't, you're right either way. It is really that simple.

A lot of times, teams think they can't win—so they don't win. And a lot of times, teams think they can win—so they do win—even though they may be less talented than the teams they beat.

I can't put my finger on it. It's not chemistry, it's not effort—it's an ingredient that I haven't been able to figure out in all my years in baseball.

But you get this feeling, like, *You know what? That other team over there is not going to beat us tonight.*

We don't have that feeling yet. At times it's been there this season, but it's not an absolute yet. It's not there on a daily or a weekly basis. But I believe it will be.

If we can get to 10 games over .500 in June and we can get on a good winning streak, then we're going to look at ourselves and say, "You know what? We are a good team."

MAY 5, 2008
DETROIT, MI

As promised, manager Jim Leyland shook things up today. The Tigers called up rookie outfielder Matt Joyce from Triple A Toledo, and Leyland moved designated hitter Gary Sheffield to left field at Sheffield's request.

"I don't know if it's going to work or not; I don't have any idea," Leyland admitted. "But I think every once in a while you have to send a message: This is a game of production. And we're not doing good enough right now.

"At some point, if the guys don't step it up, you change more personnel. If that doesn't work, at some point maybe the general manager decides to change the manager. That's the way this stuff works."

Nevertheless, it was more of the same tonight as the last-place Tigers settled for five hits, falling for the fourth game in a row, 6–3 to the Red Sox, despite a career-high eight walks courtesy of Boston's Daisuke Matsuzaka.

. . . .

Gary Sheffield came to me when we were in Minnesota over the weekend. He asked me what I thought about him going back to the outfield. I told him I thought that, physically, he could do it.

People forget that Gary has been a pretty darn good complete player for 20 years in the big leagues. He's played shortstop, he's played third base, he's played right field, he's played left field, and he's played first base. He's played a lot of different positions. He's always been on both sides of the field, offense and defense.

We're not talking about another Frank Thomas here. Frank Thomas was never anything but a hitter. He couldn't run, he couldn't throw, and he couldn't field. He never could.

With Gary Sheffield, we're talking about a guy who can still steal bases, a guy who has a real good arm, when his shoulder isn't bothering him. Gary can run and throw as well as hit. He can beat you on both sides of the field.

I told him, "Gary, if you think that you're going to be a better offensive player, if you think you're going to help this team win by playing left field, then I'm not going to disagree with you. As a matter of fact, I'll go talk to Jim Leyland about it. I'll suggest anything that you think will help you be a better baseball player." I told him, "If you think playing left field will help you be a better baseball player, then that's the most important thing."

At this point in Gary's career, if he thinks he will be a better baseball player in left field, if he thinks that will help him to be the offensive player that he wants to be and that we want him to be, then that will help the Detroit Tigers. There's no question about that.

The most important thing is for Gary Sheffield to be Gary Sheffield. Whether that means playing left field or DHing doesn't really matter.

The biggest thing for him is to stay in the game mentally. The average fan, the average person, doesn't understand what that means because they've never been on this side of the railing. They sit up in the stands and think a player's mind should work like a computer, but it doesn't. Our minds are built differently; all of our wires aren't crossed the same way. If Gary believes, in his own mind, that he will be better playing left field, then I'm all for it.

We don't know how this is going to work out—nobody does—but I totally understand Gary's position. This is a guy who, when he was DHing, didn't feel like a complete player—which, for many, many years, he was.

I understand how, especially when you are struggling with the bat, you can start to be distracted. I think, when you play defense as well as hit, it's a lot easier not to be distracted because you have to focus all the time.

When Gary was the DH, if he struck out or if he didn't get a hit, he'd have half an hour or 45 minutes before he got another turn at bat. And he'd be thinking about that last at-bat the whole time. So I'm all for this change.

But this wasn't by any means a desperation move. I don't think anything that has happened so far this year, as far as people switching positions or changes in the batting order, has been a panic move. None whatsoever.

MAY 8, 2008
DETROIT, MI
With Gary Sheffield continuing to struggle at the plate, the Tigers could definitely use another left-handed hitter, especially one with some pop in his bat. Tigers TV commentator Rod Allen, who played for the Tigers during the 1984 world championship season, told XM Radio that he thought, if something happened to Sheffield, the Tigers might be interested in signing controversial home-run king Barry Bonds, given Bonds' long relationship with Jim Leyland.

It is a provocative but intriguing thought.

. . . .

Let's say, hypothetically, Gary Sheffield breaks down physically and can't swing the bat anymore. In that case, I would have no problem at all with Barry Bonds coming here. Barry and I were teammates for six years with the Pittsburgh Pirates, and let me tell you, he is a very unique talent. Obviously, he's one of the greatest players ever to play the game.

He could show up five minutes before a game and go out and hit a two-run homer in the first inning. I couldn't do that; most guys couldn't do that. I didn't have that much talent, but Barry did. He had a switch, and he could turn it on or off.

The thing people need to understand about Barry Bonds is that, despite all of his baggage and all that other stuff, he comes to play. He comes to play every day, and I always respected that about Barry. He may not always go about his business the way I would, or the way most people would, but every night after they played that song, he was ready to play baseball.

I would go to war for Barry—at least during the game.

Back in 1988 we had a fight in the Pirates locker room one day during a rain delay. The inning before, Barry was on third base with one out and Rafael Belliard, who is now one of our Tigers coaches, was on first base, when I hit a two-hopper at Giants second baseman Robby Thompson.

Based on my speed at that time, I knew there was a good chance I was going to beat the throw. I assumed Barry was going to score on the play, and I was running as hard as I could down the line to first base to prevent the double play and allow the run to count, when all of a sudden I saw Robby Thompson throwing the ball home. I was thinking, *What is going on?*

Thompson's throw home was high, but Barry just walked right into the tag. He wasn't running hard at all, and he didn't bother to slide.

As fate would have it, we had a rain delay the next inning, so the timing was perfect. I was the first one into the locker room, and Barry was the last one in. I was waiting by his locker when he got there. Everybody in the clubhouse knew what was going to happen next. They were all watching.

Barry came strolling over to his locker and he said to me, and I'm going to quote him now, "What the f*ck do you want?"

The reality of the situation was, I wanted Barry Bonds to be a better player because I wanted us to be a better team. Believe me, it wasn't about me not getting an RBI on that play. It was all about him not utilizing the talent he was given and hurting our team. There had been other instances when Barry just hadn't put in the proper effort, and this was another one of those.

So I told him, "If you ever do that again, if you embarrass me or this team, I'm not going to wait. I'm going to kick your ass right out there on the field."

Barry pushed me, and I hit him in the face with the palm of my hand and knocked him back into his locker. I went to dive on top of him because I was going to hit him again, but I never got the chance. I was pulled off him by five or six of our pitchers. And they proceeded to do what I wanted to do: they pummeled him.

Jim Leyland was our manager. He heard the commotion and ordered both of us into his office. I went walking toward Jim's office, but when I realized Barry wasn't following me, I figured the fight was over.

Of course, that was before Barry got a whole lot bigger than me. Let me put it this way: I wouldn't have walked into that office with him in 1998. I liked my chances against him a lot better in 1988.

Having said that, if one of the players on the other team had challenged Barry Bonds on the field that day, I would have been there to defend him, because he was a teammate.

He came to play and he came to beat the other team—most of the time, anyway.

MAY 13, 2008
KANSAS CITY, MO

Rookie Matt Joyce gave the Tigers a two-run lead in the second inning tonight with his second home run in two games, but that was the end of their offense as they succumbed, 3–2, to the Kansas City Royals. The Tigers collected nine hits but stranded nine potential runs on the base paths.

"Everybody talks about on-base percentage, but I like slugging percentage," Jim Leyland said afterward. "Normally, during the course of a game, there are going to be enough guys on base. The key is to knock 'em in."

•   •   •   •

It's no secret we needed another left-handed bat. And Matt Joyce, who didn't get much attention during spring training, has been a pleasant surprise in our lineup. He's provided a little spark at times.

Remember, Albert Pujols wasn't supposed to be such a good player coming out of spring training a few years ago, either. And look how good he turned out to be. I'm not saying Matt Joyce is another Albert Pujols, but now and then you get these surprises and you ride 'em as long as you can. Who knows? We may ride Matt Joyce for 10 years. You never know.

With kids like Joyce, I try to talk to them on a regular basis about the mental part of the game. I can remember, when I was 25 years old, thinking I had all the answers. And when I got to be 35, and I finally started to figure out that I didn't know everything, I wished I still had the body I had when I was 25. I talk to Joyce and I talk to the other young guys about how to play the right way. That's all you can do. You show them the right way to do things. Then they have to go out and get it done.

The thing about coaching is you have to speak differently to every player. You can't speak the same language about the same thing to every player. They're all different, so you have to communicate in different ways. Sometimes it's with a few words, but a lot of times it's with a long dissertation.

Tonight against Kansas City, Nate Robertson made one bad pitch to the Royals' Jose Guillen, Edgar Renteria made one error, and it cost us the ballgame. We lost a game that way in Minnesota, too.

If we were going good, and Jose Guillen would have popped that pitch up tonight, and Renteria would have made a perfect flip to Placido Polanco at second base, then it would still have been a tie game that we probably could have won in the ninth or tenth inning.

There is a psychological thing about waiting for the other shoe to fall. There are times, when we're losing like this, where I find myself thinking, *I've got a bad feeling about this. I don't like this pitch in this situation.*

But when we are winning, it's just the opposite. I'm thinking, *This guy is going to make a perfect pitch,* or *Even if our pitcher does make a mistake, this guy isn't going to hit it anyway.*

Whether you think you can or you think you can't does make a difference; I really believe in that. If you think you can do something, you can do it. And if you think you can't do something, you can't. Right now, I think we're convincing ourselves that we can't.

I remember us being a real good team for the first year and half that I was a Tigers coach. So one of the things I did when I went home to St. Louis on the off-day on Monday was go on my computer and look back at last year.

On July 23, 2007, we were 21 games over .500. We are now 17 games under .500. And in that span, the ERA of our starting pitchers has been 5.61. That is the story right there; that's the whole story. A team can't win when your starting pitchers have an ERA of 5.61. You just can't.

I'm not blaming the starting pitchers. But that is the reality of what has happened over almost a full calendar year. As good an offense as we have had since I've been here, unless you are always on top of your game offensively, you can't overcome that kind of pitching. And it's impossible—impossible—for a major-league team to always be on top of its game offensively. You just can't do it.

Major-league hitters cannot continue to play at their highest levels all the time. That's just the reality of the game. You're going to run into hot pitchers, and hitters are going to have slumps.

Having said all of that, right now we are in a situation where our starting pitchers are struggling and we've got hitters who are not performing up to expectations. That's a dangerous combination. They know it; we all know it. That's just where we are right now.

How do we get out of that funk? There are no answers. There's not a manager or a coach or a general manager who has the answer to what is going on here right now. You are at the mercy of the players you put on the field. And right now, we all know we're not playing at a high level.

But it's still going to happen, I think. Hopefully it will happen sooner rather than later, because if it doesn't, we're going to find ourselves in a place it will be really hard to come back from.

MAY 14, 2008
KANSAS CITY, MO

Justin Verlander saw his record drop to 1–7 tonight, even though he again pitched well enough to win. The Tigers were held to six singles and shut out for the sixth time, 2–0 by the Royals. It marked the 21st time in 40 games that the Tigers have failed to win while scoring four runs or fewer. With nearly a quarter of the season in the books, they have yet to win a low-scoring game.

"We should not get shut out," Jim Leyland admitted matter-of-factly. "It's not a matter of bad luck. Things aren't going against us. We're not making enough good things happen. We're doing all the things to lose games instead of things to win games."

In Verlander's seven losses, his teammates have scored a total of just two runs while he was actually on the mound and have been outscored 48–7 overall.

．　　．　　．　　．

We left eight guys on base tonight. Last night we left nine guys on base. The other day we left 11. I think we left 14 one night when we lost a game. That's the offense's fault. But everyone's at fault—I'm at fault, the other coaches are at fault, the manager is at fault, and the players are at fault.

One of the things that really ticks me off is when I hear that there is pressure on Jim Leyland or on the pitching coach, Chuck Hernandez, or on the hitting coach, Lloyd McClendon.

You know what? When I first came here, for the first year and half, throughout 2006 and for the first half of 2007, there was less coaching and less managing going on than there has been for the last year and a half. That was because we were winning. When you're winning, you stay out of the way of a horse that's out in front. You let that horse run.

What do you think happens to a horse that is falling behind halfway through the Kentucky Derby? He gets whipped in the rear end. In a sense, if we as coaches and managers are guilty of anything, we're probably guilty of whipping the players harder than we did when we first got here in 2006.

Touted as a preseason Cy Young Award candidate and potential 20-game winner, Justin Verlander instead led all American League pitchers in losses with 17. He suffered from a lack of support early on as the Tigers were outscored 48–7 in Verlander's first seven defeats.

We're trying harder. We're looking at more video tape. We've taken more early batting practice already this year in the first six weeks of the season than we did in the first two seasons I was here. It's not even two months into the season and we've already taken more extra hitting than we did in the last two years combined. So it isn't a matter of not working. Believe me, the work is taking place.

I don't know what the answer is. There is no answer. If we knew the answer, we would do it. If I knew the answer, I wouldn't be coaching first base for the Detroit Tigers; I would be consulting with every team that wasn't playing winning baseball. And I'd be making a lot of money.

MAY 15, 2008
KANSAS CITY, MO

I cooled my heels in the hallway outside the Tigers' locker room for 25 minutes this morning while the players, who are as perplexed as everyone else about the way this season is unraveling, held a closed-door players-only meeting.

Then they proceeded to hit a new low in the Jim Leyland Era, bowing 8–4 to the Royals to fall nine games under .500 for the first time since September 2005, before Alan Trammell was fired as the Tigers' manager.

"Guys just wanted to sit down and figure it out," explained closer Todd Jones after the clubhouse doors reopened. "A lot of times, when you hear it from guys on the team, it holds a lot more importance than when it comes from other people.

"It's like rehab. You have to acknowledge things. That's the first step. I guess we have to figure it out."

"We wanted to reinforce what this team can be," said pitcher Kenny Rogers, another grizzled veteran. "We know how good we are. We can be as good as we want to be. We need to stop worrying about what we're supposed to be. We've been a winning club before, and we will be again."

"I'm puzzled by the inconsistency of our offense," manager Jim Leyland admitted.

"Our bats look like they're dragging, like they weigh 10 pounds. We can't be tired. We just had two days off. If we've got guys who are tired now, we've got a major problem."

.   .   .   .

We should have won at least two of the three games here in Kansas City this week. But we didn't; we lost all three. The whole series was typical of our season so far. We're losing games that we were winning during the previous two years.

We didn't get any big hits or any hits with men in scoring position. When that starts happening, as a player, it's like being inside a pressure cooker. The longer you feel the heat, the more the pressure builds. Until somebody blows the lid off—and that sometimes only takes one player—the pressure keeps building.

That's just human nature. A player can say all the right things and he can think all the right things. But until somebody executes, until one player helps his team break out, until one player or several players get hot—and getting hot can mean just getting one big hit for three or four games in a row—the pressure keeps building. You could feel that happening during all three games here in Kansas City.

It doesn't take three or four hits in a game to break out of it. Sometimes, it just takes that one big hit—a two-out single with men on base or that run-clearing double. That relaxes everybody and gets everybody thinking, *Now I don't have to do it* or *I don't have to get it done right now in this at-bat.* Then everybody feels like the pressure is off them.

But as long as that pressure is on, from my experience, it leads to a lot of failure. There's nothing in life that you can do well when you're under a lot of pressure, mentally and physically. In everybody's lives, not just ballplayers', mental pressure can lead to all sorts of problems, such as high stress or heart trouble.

In this game, you can have physical pressure along with that mental pressure—pressure to hit, pressure to pitch, pressure to field. And in baseball, unlike in other sports, there are very few ways of releasing that pressure.

In hockey, you can skate down the ice and check somebody. In football, you can run down the field and hit somebody. In basketball, you run up and down the court and expel a lot of energy that way. But in baseball, you sit around and you think, and you feel, and the pressure mounts.

The average fan does not understand the mental pressure that can build up in a player during the course of a game, during the course of a series, and certainly over the course of a season, when things are not going well.

MAY 20, 2008
DETROIT, MI

Visibly angry over an article in *USA Today* that painted an unfavorable picture of the atmosphere inside the Tigers' clubhouse, including quotes from Carlos

Guillen and Brandon Inge as well as former Tigers pitcher Jason Grilli, who described that atmosphere as "stale and stagnant," Jim Leyland closed the doors to the locker room for 20 minutes before batting practice tonight and ordered his players to "look in the mirror."

Leyland banned card-playing and ordered the half-dozen TV sets in the clubhouse turned off except for video of that particular day's opposing pitcher. He also barred the players' kids and family members from the locker room.

It was a vintage Leyland tirade, his biggest explosion since he took over as the Tigers' manager in 2006.

"Those are diversionary tactics," Leyland charged, referring to the players' comments that were cited in the article. "That's all bullshit.

"I can take the heat, and I deserve some for the performance of this club. But there are some players in that clubhouse who need to look in the mirror, too. Don't look in my mirror. Look in their own mirrors.

"When people start making weak excuses in the newspaper, that rubs me the wrong way. The problem here is between the lines. That's where the problem lies.

"Everybody is looking for excuses," Leyland said. "And to me that's weak shit. Weak! If a player doesn't like what is going on in the clubhouse, put a name to it. Stick your chest out and put a name to it.

"The last thing they should be doing is popping off to the newspapers," Leyland continued. "If you're hitting .200, you shouldn't be popping off.

"If the players want to start talking, then I'll start talking," Leyland warned. "If they want to play games in the press, then I'll play games in the press. And, trust me, it won't be very pretty.

"I'll put names to it. I'll quit protecting guys night after night after night."

"Some guys in here just can't keep their mouth[s] shut," closer Todd Jones told me after things had quieted down. "They're going to spoil it for everybody.

"They've got to remember, this guy [Leyland] took on Barry Bonds in Pittsburgh," Jones said softly. "You don't mess with him. He won't put up with it."

. . . .

We had a team meeting tonight and, really, for the first time since Jim Leyland has been here, he laid everything on the line. It was a very, very explosive meeting, and rightfully so. It was the old Jim Leyland that I remember from when I played for him in Pittsburgh.

Meetings like this are supposed to stay in the clubhouse. They're supposed to be between the manager and the coaches and the players only, so I've got to be very careful about what I say. But I will say this much: tonight's meeting was very, very apropos. It was very much needed.

Jim is mad and frustrated. He said he wanted everybody—including me, all of the players, all of the coaches, and even himself—to look in the mirror and stop pointing fingers. As usual, Jim being Jim, he took most of the blame, but he also wanted everybody in the room to know he's not solely responsible for what is going on around here.

Everybody on this team is responsible for our failure so far, just like everybody on the team was responsible in 2006 and for the first four months of last season when we were winning.

Good players point the finger at themselves when things are going bad and point the finger at others when things are going well.

MAY 22, 2008
DETROIT, MI

The players' kids were back in the clubhouse today, but the big-screen TV sets remained dark, and there were no card games as the Tigers completed a three-game sweep of the struggling Seattle Mariners, 9–2.

Three games, 30 runs, 44 hits, three wins—it's amazing what a spurt like that will do for a team's morale—even a last-place team like the Tigers.

If it is true, as Brandon Inge suggested after today's game, that Tuesday's fiery pregame lecture from Jim Leyland represented "the lowest point of our season," then this hit-filled three-game sweep of the Mariners represented one of the high points so far.

"Sometimes you've got to hit rock bottom before you can refocus and say, 'This is ridiculous,'" admitted Inge, who homered for his third extra-base hit in two days. "It's good to get some wins and refocus the feeling in here on the fact that we really are a good team.

"There was so much negative exposure that all of a sudden every loss was magnified. It's easy to let all the negatives get you down.

"That should have been a gut-check for everybody," Inge continued, referring to Leyland's "Look in the mirror" rant. "Sitting in our chairs, listening to him, everybody in this locker room should have been trying to figure out how to make this team better instead of being quoted in newspaper articles.

"What I'm seeing now are guys who know it's time to step it up. I can't speak for everyone, but it seems like everybody was battling during this series. It seemed like our at-bats were more angry. It felt like they were more focused and aggressive.

"The only thing you can control in this entire game is how hard you play," Inge added. "Once you dedicate yourself to playing as hard as you can, that's when good things happen. That's when you make the plays."

.   .   .   .

During the last three games, against Seattle, we finally played the way everybody has expected us to play since the season began. It's true, some of Seattle's pitchers had some high ERAs coming into the series, and we took advantage of those pitchers who were struggling a little bit. But that's what good teams are supposed to do. Even when your opponent is struggling, you've still got to go out there on the field and beat them. Wins don't automatically happen just because the other team is doing bad. You've still got to hit the ball and pitch. If you don't, I guarantee they'll beat you. We've got to win more series like this if we want to be in the pennant race come September.

I think this sweep helped the ballclub psychologically more than anything else. Our offense looks like it's going to start jelling. We got some hits with runners in scoring position, and that's something we haven't been doing. We had some sustained rallies, which is good. We got some hits with two outs.

I don't know if I'd say we were fed up with losing. But a lot of times, frustration leads to doubt, and doubt is the worst thing you can have in any sport. When you're playing golf, if you have doubt in your mind when you're standing over a three-foot putt, you're not going to make it. If you have doubt before you step in the batter's box, your chances go way, way down.

I'm a big body-language guy, I really am. And, more than anything else, it looks like our body language is getting better. There seems to be less stress in our players' bodies than I was seeing before. All body language is really, is a mirror of what is going on in your brain, because whatever is going on in your brain will seep out through your body.

Last weekend, in Arizona, it was just the opposite. Look at our first inning on Sunday against Randy Johnson. Sure, he shut us out. But we had a nice rally going in that first inning and we had the guy we wanted, Magglio Ordonez, at the plate. I'm not criticizing Magglio; that was just the reality. He hit the ball hard, but it was right at the Diamondbacks' second baseman for an easy double play.

Last year or two years ago, that ball would have gone through for a double, and we would have been up 2–0. We would have been off and rolling, and it would have been a different ballgame. But so far this year, there have been very few games when we have come right out of the gate and jumped out to a nice lead.

I don't know what the statistics are, but I know they must be really, really high, that the team that scores two or three runs in the first inning goes on to win the ballgame.

MAY 25, 2008
DETROIT, MI

It continues to be feast or famine with these Tigers. Last night they mauled the Minnesota Twins 19–3. This afternoon, some 12 hours later, they had all that they could do to score one run.

Nevertheless, Jim Leyland was surprisingly upbeat—not only about the fact that Justin Verlander, who has been working with pitching coach Chuck

Hernandez on his mechanics and his delivery, reached 99 mph on the radar gun for the first time this year. Leylad is happy about the way the Tigers hitters are swinging the bats, at least some of the time.

"That's the Justin Verlander I've been looking for; that's the Justin Verlander we know," Leyland raved after the game, an otherwise lackluster 6–1 loss to the Twins that left the Tigers with a 4–2 record on this homestand.

Leyland is a realist. He knows the Tigers can't make up for two mystifyingly miserable months in one series or one homestand.

"We've got to crawl back into contention," Leyland said today, well aware that won't be easy so long as the White Sox keep winning. "Creep and crawl, that's what we've got to do. Pick up a game here and pick up a game there. Try to win two out of three in every series and get back to respectability." Nevertheless, privately Leyland is not happy about the way his high-powered, high-priced lineup has repeatedly been rendered helpless by the likes of Minnesota's Kevin Slowey and Glen Perkins—pitchers that they, by rights, ought to pulverize.

In their four wins on this homestand, the Tigers banged out 61 hits and scored 49 runs. In their two losses to the Twins, they scored just five.

So far this season, when they score five runs or more, the Tigers are 20–3. But they are 1–26 when they score four or less.

Obviously, the secret is to score at least five runs.

.   .   .   .

The best thing is that I haven't seen our hitters give in. That's the big thing. They haven't given in. Sometimes their approach at the plate hasn't made the manager or the hitting coach happy. But they're not giving in. Having a bad approach and giving in are two different things.

I threw batting practice again before today's game. I usually throw about 20 minutes, but I've thrown up to an hour of BP. That's a big part of my job that nobody except the players ever sees. My BP is different than the BP that the other Tigers coaches throw. I throw very hard BP that is more equivalent to game-speed pitching.

I stand 10 feet closer to the plate than the pitchers do during the actual games. So when I throw in the 70s, it is the equivalent of about 90 miles an hour because I'm only 50 feet away. That 10 feet makes a big difference

Some guys like it, and some guys don't. I'm here for the guys who want to duplicate game-speed pitching in practice as much as possible. When a coach is throwing batting practice at 50 miles per hour, a hitter can take a pitch that's three or four inches off the plate and do whatever he wants to do with it. If it's outside, he can hit it the opposite way, and if it's inside, he can hit it out of the ballpark.

When I'm throwing, the hitters can't do that. It's more like game conditions.

MAY 31, 2008
SEATTLE, WA

Jim Leyland tweaked the starting lineup again today, but the result was another loss, 5–0 to the lowly Seattle Mariners. It was the Tigers' ninth whitewash of the year, the worst such mark in the American League.

"If you go to the lake for two straight weeks and never get a bite, you go to a different lake," the Tigers' manager said in explaining his decision to play Curtis Granderson against left-handed pitchers even though the left-hand–hitting

Granderson has struggled against lefties in the past. This was also how he explained his decision to play Marcus Thames regularly in left field, even though Thames has historically had trouble with right-handers.

"The observations and analysis are over. It's time for production," Leyland declared.

"You've got some track records, and obviously you go with that and don't panic," Leyland said of his hitters. "But at some point the track record has got to do something, or you look for somebody else to play. You look for guys who are going to give you your best shot.

"I don't want to be patient to a fault. It's almost June and things haven't worked very well. I can't just sit here. If you don't do something, I think you're foolish as a manager. We've got an owner who has too much invested. My general manager has given me a hell of a team here. I haven't really coached it to the right flow.

"As a manager, you can't be afraid to try things. If you are, you might as well go home. We need to go with what gives [us] the best shot right now.

"I'm not going to give up until we get it right," Leyland added. "I'm going to work my butt off. I'm going to change some things around here and see what happens. I don't know if it's going to work or make people angry, but that's the way it goes. We are beyond feelings around here; we're beyond worrying about egos.

"I'm not down on anybody. This is just tinkering, not a panic. This is about doing the job. We have to get it rolling somehow."

Leyland suspects Granderson's hand, which he broke when he was hit by a pitch during spring training, may still be bothering him. However, Granderson said again today that his hand is fine.

"Put him up there. Let's find out. It's time to find out," Leyland said of Granderson. "He's the guy who gives us speed up top. If he gets on, he can generate a run sometimes with his legs. Curtis Granderson is going to be a great player, and I can't hide from the fact that he's our catalyst."

Granderson is hitting .295 in his career against right-handers and .201 against left-handers.

"Marcus Thames deserves a shot," Leyland said, explaining his decision to play Thames full-time. "Marcus can be a streaky guy, and hopefully we can get him on a streak. If he can start hitting some three-run homers, that would be a big thing for us. I've got to try something."

. . . .

We got beat today by Seattle's Felix Hernandez, who is capable of shutting down any team.

Having said that, we could have won this game. We got two guys on with one out in the first inning against Hernandez, and we couldn't score. Both Magglio Ordonez and Marcus Thames struck out. We didn't take advantage of our situation or of Hernandez's state of mind. We couldn't get a runner to second base the rest of the game. Hernandez has had the worst run support of any starter in the American League this season, and we let him off the hook.

At this level, the team that scores first is going to win 60 percent of the time.

And Hernandez is the type of kid you can unnerve. At this point in his career, in my opinion, he's not the type of guy who's going to fight back. But he ended up shutting us down on two hits—two singles! It was another opportunity that we let get away, which has been going on a lot this year.

I think Jim's decision to play Curtis Granderson more was a good one. I've said it before, and I'll keep saying it: Curtis Granderson is the most important part of this offense. When he goes, we'll go. And except for that first week or so when he came back from his broken hand, he hasn't been going.

I don't know if it is a residual effect of him breaking his hand in spring training, I don't know if it's mechanical, I don't know the reason, but he certainly hasn't been a consistent part of our offense.

I still believe Curtis is going to be the most important part of the equation the rest of the year for us. He's got to be the guy who takes us to the next level. We are not going to get back to .500 until Curtis starts hitting.

Chapter 5

JUNE

"We're Supposed to Be Good"

JUNE 1, 2008
SEATTLE, WA

 "Play a full nine innings." That is the slogan that is forever etched inside the Tigers' 2006 American League championship rings. And that is the mantra Jim Leyland has preached since the day he arrived in Detroit. Today, for a change, the Tigers played a full nine innings, grinding out a 7–5 victory with four runs in the ninth inning to take two out of three from the hapless Mariners.

It was the Tigers' biggest ninth inning yet this season—nearly matching the incredibly feeble total of just five runs that they managed to score during all of their previous ninth innings combined during the first two dismal months of the season.

It was a welcome change after incurring two shutouts in the first six games of this road trip. "We just keep creeping along," Jim Leyland said.

. . . .

We came to Seattle and we played good, winning two out of three, which is what we should do against a team that is struggling the way the Mariners are. But we could be riding a six-game winning streak right now. Instead, we're 3–3.

Curtis Granderson stole a base today, the first one we've stolen in more than three weeks. I don't do it very often, but sometimes I'll give the steal sign from the first-base coach's box instead of having the runner get it from Gene Lamont over at third.

It's usually not even a sign. I'll usually just step over and talk to the runner quietly, so the first baseman can't hear what I'm saying, of course.

If I think a pitcher is tipping off the fact that he is going to throw home, or if I see a catcher setting up a certain way on a particular pitch, I'll let the runner know that he should be ready to go.

Sometimes I can see the pitcher gripping the ball a certain way and I can tell the next pitch is going to be a change-up or a curveball. Well, if that pitcher is 1.4 seconds to the plate with his fast ball, I know he's going to 1.5 or 1.6 seconds with a change or a curveball. Then I may just wink, or I may say something to the runner like, "OK, let's go," and he knows what I mean.

I'm always looking for an opportunity for a guy like Pudge Rodriguez or Carlos Guillen or, of course, Curtis, to run. Those guys have enough speed that, if the pitcher is giving away something, we can take advantage of it.

Like I said, I don't do that very often. The situation has to be right. If the hitter at the plate is hot or if he has good numbers against this pitcher, there's no reason to take any unnecessary chances by running. But if the hitter at the plate is not swinging the bat well or if he's got the count against him, like 1–2, then sometimes I'll take a shot.

JUNE 4, 2008
OAKLAND, CA

After two walk-off losses in a row, the Tigers were walloped, 10–2, by the Oakland A's this afternoon.

"Our offense basically has stunk," Jim Leyland admitted. "I'm sorry. That's just the way it is. I'm befuddled."

One thing Leyland hates to hear is a reporter asking about the so-called "chemistry" in the struggling Tigers' clubhouse.

"I'm so sick of hearing about team chemistry, I'm never going to talk about it again—ever in my life," the manager bristled. "When it gets brought up, I'm going to say, 'Next question.'

"It makes me sick. I can't stand it. It has nothing to do with anything. When you win, the chemistry is good. When you lose, the chemistry is bad.

"I don't care if players get into a fistfight," Leyland continued. "I read today that Lou Gehrig and Babe Ruth didn't like each other. Well, they won a lot of games.

"Give me talent. I don't care if they fight for 21 hours a day. For three hours, go out and beat somebody."

. . . .

We got to Oakland and the same darn thing happened again. Just like in Anaheim, we should have won the first two games here against the A's. Instead, we ended up losing, 3–2 and 5–4, in walk-off situations because we didn't take advantage of our scoring opportunities earlier in the game. Again, we couldn't drive in guys from third base. That's one of the things that's been killing us. Then today we got blown out, 10–2.

The interesting thing about this road trip is that I thought we pitched as well as we have all year. The pitching was really good. But our offense, for some reason, is still mired in a team slump. We haven't had one guy bust out and carry us. I've been saying that for two months now, and it still hasn't happened.

We've had four walk-off losses in eight games on this road trip. You just don't see that; even on bad teams you don't see that, and we are supposed to be a good team. Usually when that happens, it's the little things that are getting you beat.

We had a guy, Clete Thomas, thrown out at home. He was probably safe, I thought he was, but the umpire saw it differently. If we were winning, we probably would have gotten that call and Thomas would have scored. That's what happens when you're going bad.

Then when we had the opportunity to throw somebody out at home ourselves, Pudge Rodriguez dropped the ball. How often does that happen? I'm not pointing fingers at anybody; that's just the way things are going right now. We are just not making plays. We're not making pitches when we need to make pitches, and we're not getting hits when we need to get hits.

Losing like we did in the first two games here in Oakland, in the other team's last at-bat, is always rough. But when you're struggling the way we are, when you're not winning, it's like rubbing salt in your wounds.

You get involved in a game where you're finally competing, you finally feel like you've got a good chance to win, and then, at the last minute, you lose again.

We are now 1–32 when we have scored four runs or fewer. 1–32! Think about that. That's unreal! And we've been shut out nine times. Last year, we only got shut out three times all year. Statistically, it just doesn't add up that this ball team could be 1–32 when scoring four runs or fewer, with nine shutouts—and we're not halfway through June yet. That's unbelievable.

At least we're going bad together. We're going bad as a team. I guess that should be some consolation.

JUNE 7, 2008
DETROIT, MI

Jeremy Bonderman's jersey hung from a hanger taped to the roof of the Tigers' dugout for all to see during this afternoon's game. It was a grim reminder of the latest obstacle in this supposed dream season, a season that has so far been a nightmare.

When Bonderman reported to Comerica Park yesterday afternoon, his right shoulder, which had felt heavy and achy for a couple of days, was visibly swollen. The 25-year-old right hander was sent to the hospital where doctors discovered a blood clot and performed two emergency surgical procedures last night and this morning to remove the blockage.

Bonderman will undergo further examinations, but he will probably have to have surgery to remove the first rib on his right side, which means he will be lost for the season.

Bonderman, looking tired but relieved, was released from the hospital late this afternoon and returned to the ballpark in time to watch the end of the Tigers' 8–4 win over the Cleveland Indians.

"I'm not dead yet," he joked, forcing a weak smile. "It's scary, but it's nice to know they can figure out a way to keep it from happening again."

Bonderman's teammates were shaken by the news.

"When you hear blood clot, you think, *That's serious. You can die from that*," Brandon Inge said.

"As a friend, I'm glad they caught it," Justin Verlander said. "But as a teammate, it's pretty upsetting to know he's not going to be around for a while. It's a huge blow to our team. It definitely was a shock. You don't expect something like that. He pitched last Sunday and then, *bam!* Blood clot. You're done."

Bonderman, whose performance on the mound had improved of late, was 3–4 with a 4.29 ERA. He signed a four-year, $38 million contract prior to the 2007 season.

This marks the second time in 15 months that a member of the Tigers' starting rotation has been sidelined by a blood clot. Veteran left-hander Kenny Rogers missed the first three months of the 2007 season after undergoing surgery to remove a clot and repair the arteries in his pitching shoulder.

"He's lucky. Something like this can be lethal," said Rogers, who also had his first rib removed five or six years ago. "Now he'll be able to do things he wanted to do but couldn't."

According to Tigers head athletic trainer Kevin Rand, Bonderman's clot was in a vein that carries blood from his shoulder back to his heart. Rogers' clot was in an artery carrying blood to his arm.

Rand said in both cases the clots were probably caused by the unnatural motion of throwing a baseball overhand. "You and I, the average person on the street, are not at risk for something like this," Rand explained.

"We've been fighting through a lot of stuff. It's been one thing after another," admitted Jim Leyland. "In situations like this, you find out how tough you are."

"It'll be just one more chapter in the greatest comeback in baseball history," predicted closer Todd Jones, who has always had a flair for the dramatic.

.   .   .   .

This is a huge loss for our team. It's hard to replace a guy you are counting on to go out and give you 220 or 240 innings. This is about more than just Jeremy's wins or his losses or his ERA. It's about giving our bullpen a rest, and Jeremy is the type of guy who does that for his team. You always knew he was going to give 100 percent, even when he got beat. We saw that in California on the last road trip, when he didn't want to come out of the game. That's the kind of stuff you can't replace.

On top of that, Bondo is a good guy; everybody likes him. When you lose a guy with that kind of personality, a guy who can give you innings, it's a big blow to any team—especially one that is struggling the way we are right now. But it can also serve as a rallying cry for the rest of the team.

If we're going to get back into this thing, losing one guy—even a guy as valuable as Bondo—is not a crutch that we should be leaning on.

Our hitting has been better lately, and our pitching has kept us in games. But offensively, we're still not where we should be.

Our record is what it is. We've still only won one game when we've scored four runs or fewer.

JUNE 10, 2008
DETROIT, MI

After watching Dontrelle Willis walk five batters and give up eight runs in 1⅓ erratic innings in last night's 8–2 loss to the Cleveland Indians, the Tigers moved quickly today, optioning the 26-year-old left-hander to their Class A Lakeland, Florida, farm club, where he will work, until further notice, on his mechanics and his mental state—well away from the media spotlight. The Tigers brass had seen enough.

The Tigers knew Willis had been experiencing control problems when they traded prize prospects Andrew Miller and Cameron Maybin plus four others to the Florida Marlins for Dontrelle and Miguel Cabrera last December.

They knew Willis had walked a career-high 87 batters in 205 innings with the Marlins last season when they signed him to a three-year $29 million contract this winter. But they also knew he was a 22-game winner and an All-Star three years ago.

"We studied it thoroughly at the time we made the trade," said Tigers president and general manager Dave Dombrowski today.

"Our objective is to get Dontrelle back to being Dontrelle—the Dontrelle that we know," Dombrowski explained. "We want to get him back to being the

Dontrelle he has been in the past, get him back to being an effective major-league pitcher."

With the loss of Jeremy Bonderman because of a blood clot in his shoulder, the Tigers are now minus two of their five starting pitchers—at a time when they need all of the help they can get.

"My heart is broken for the kid," admitted Jim Leyland, who spent the night at the ballpark, sleeping in his office, after the Tigers' latest loss. "My heart ached for him last night. I love him. He's a stand-up guy. He wants to compete."

But Willis' 21 walks, 13 runs, and 10.32 ERA after four abbreviated starts left the Tigers with little choice.

Under baseball rules, Willis, as a veteran, had to agree to his minor-league assignment. "He knew he wasn't doing well and didn't want to hurt his team," Dombrowski explained.

A few hours after Willis departed, the Tigers commenced a critical three-game series against the Chicago White Sox, who swept them in Detroit during the winless first week of the season and took two of three from them the following weekend in Chicago.

This time, with their season possibly on the line, the Tigers prevailed, 6–4, as Miguel Cabrera collected three hits and knocked in a couple of runs.

.   .   .   .

This was a big win for us. When we took the field tonight, trailing Chicago by 10½ games in the standings, we were thinking, *Wait a minute. Are the White Sox really that much better than us?*

We don't believe that. Sure, they are pitching better, their bullpen is really good, and they've hit more home runs than we have. But they're certainly not scoring more runs than us.

They're healthy, and when you're healthy, a lot of times that's as important as having talent.

I was thinking to myself before the game, *Yeah, they're a good club, but so are we. They're just playing better than we are right now. They're winning the games that we're not.* However, it's one thing to think that way and another to do something about it.

After tonight's game we looked across the field at the White Sox bench, and I know every one of us said to ourselves, "They're not better than us."

After losing Jeremy Bonderman and now losing Dontrelle Willis for a while, too—two of our five starters—this win was huge for us psychologically. We needed to show that we aren't going to let losing those two guys get us down.

Last night's game against Cleveland, with Willis pitching, was ugly. I don't think anybody could have felt worse for somebody than we did for Dontrelle. That was really hard to watch. We felt terrible for him. That was the feeling that permeated the bench during those first two innings while Dontrelle was on the mound.

We didn't feel bad for ourselves, even though we realized, obviously, the way he started off, we were probably going to wind up losing the game. We just felt bad for him. Regardless of whether you like a guy or don't like a guy, regardless of whether he's on your team or on the other team, you hate to see a professional athlete go through an embarrassment like that.

Jim Leyland tried everything he could to change things mentally for Dontrelle. Pitching coach Chuck Hernandez did everything mechanically that he could do. But nothing went right.

I don't think Dontrelle has the same problem Steve Blass had with the Pirates back in the early 1970s or the same problem Rick Ankiel had with the Cardinals before he moved to the outfield. There's something else going on with Dontrelle. The wires between his brain and his arm have somehow gotten crossed. There's a connection there that's not working right, for some reason. And Dontrelle is the one who is ultimately going to be responsible for fixing it.

JUNE 11, 2008
DETROIT, MI

Pitching on the eve of the anniversary of his spectacular no-hitter last season, Justin Verlander delivered the type of performance the Tigers have been waiting all year to see as he held the surprising first-place Chicago White Sox to four hits for a 5–1 win.

It was the first complete game by a Tigers pitcher since Verlander's gem against the Milwaukee Brewers a year ago.

"Wouldn't that have been something?" said Verlander, who claimed he wasn't even aware of the anniversary until after the game. "It wasn't quite the same, but I'll take it."

So, under current circumstances, will the Tigers.

· · · ·

As I said before, the White Sox are the one team in the American League that we most want to beat. I think, in part, it's because we know they're going to be good. That's No. 1. And they've been there, they won the world championship three years ago, so they know how to win. To be the best, you have to beat the best teams in your division. But mostly I think it's just the whole persona of the White Sox that makes us want to beat them.

It's nothing personal. The White Sox are not bad guys. I like a lot of them personally, but there's a certain persona that exudes from them that just makes you want to beat them. I think its a derivative of Ozzie Guillen, their manager, and his personality. Ozzie doesn't have a bad personality, but you never know what he's going to do. You never know what he's going to say. In a lot of ways, it's kind of an entertaining personality. And in a lot of ways, it can be annoying. That makes it more exciting, more fun, when you beat him.

It's probably like beating the New York Yankees was when Billy Martin was their manager or beating the Tigers when Martin was managing here.

There are some guys you just want to beat. Ozzie Guillen is one of those guys. I think that's good.

I had a little incident of my own with him. At the beginning of last year, I was watching on TV when Ozzie took out a pitcher; I think it was a rookie pitcher. They apparently had some issues. I don't know if Ozzie had ordered the kid to hit somebody or what. It wasn't a game against us.

Anyway, Ozzie just lit into him on the bench. Some writer from Chicago asked me about it later, and I said, "I know if I was playing, I wouldn't like that. And if I was managing, I wouldn't treat my players like that." That was all I said.

But that's Ozzie. The same thing that makes him great can also make him vulnerable to criticism.

All I told the reporter was, "I don't buy into this 'atypical Latin temper' stuff." Well, when it came out, I was quoted as saying, "Ozzie has a typical Latin temper." That pissed Ozzie off. But that wasn't what I said. What I actually said was, "He is not a typical Latin. He's atypical."

Anyway, Ozzie got all out of whack. He made some derogatory statements toward me, about how he'd be managing in the big leagues long after I wasn't coaching first base in the big leagues anymore. I never made a rebuttal because I didn't think it was any big deal. It certainly was not a big deal to me. In fact, what he said may be true. It probably will be true. Ozzie will probably be managing long after I'm not coaching anymore.

But that doesn't make him a better guy.

JUNE 12, 2008
DETROIT, MI

The Tigers completed an unexpected but much-needed sweep over the White Sox with a 2–1 win this afternoon, thanks to Miguel Cabrera's walk-off, wrong-field home run to right in the bottom of the ninth—Cabrera's biggest hit yet as a Tiger.

This is just the second time all season that the Tigers have succeeded when scoring four runs or fewer and their first when scoring just two runs.

Kenny Rogers pitched about as well as a 43-year-old left-hander can pitch, holding the division-leading ChiSox to one run on four hits over the first eight innings. Although he didn't get credit for the victory, Rogers called it, "A building-block game."

"Winning close, low-scoring games like this is the only thing that is going to get us back into the race," Rogers declared. "Winning games like this is what is going to give us confidence. We can't count on the offense. We can't rely on anything but pitching and defense. If we can win some of these things, it will relax us."

"We need to win some games, 1–0 and 2–1, to take some of the heat, some of the presumed blame, off the hitters," agreed closer Todd Jones, who picked up his second win along with 11 saves.

Jim Leyland called the victory "a baby step."

"I think we took three baby steps this week," he said. "That's what we need to do right now. There's time enough to walk later. There's no need for a sprint."

·　·　·　·

Psychologically, I think we went over a big hurdle this afternoon.

I said before this series started that this was going to be our testing ground, that these three games against the White Sox were either going to make or break our season, not so much statistically as mentally. I think, psychologically, these guys had to prove to themselves that, no matter what our record said, no matter what the standings said, the White Sox weren't any better than us.

I don't want to say it was a "must-sweep" because I don't think that was the case. But we certainly needed to win two of the three games, and there was no way—no way—we could have afforded to lose all three. That would have put us 13½ games behind Chicago and 14 games under .500, and we would have been thinking, *Maybe they are that much better than us after all.*

Instead, we're 7½ games back and eight under. For these three games anyway, we proved to ourselves, and to the White Sox, that we can play better than them. That is the only way we can get back in this thing—we have to win series after series. We don't have to sweep everybody, but we have to win at least two out of every three. And we have to play well when we're doing it. This is the first time in a while that we've played well for a whole series.

Everybody will talk about Marcus Thames' three-run homer in the second game and the walk-off homer from Miguel Cabrera in the bottom of the ninth today, but the key to this series was our pitching. We got good pitching all three games—from Nate Robertson, from Justin Verlander, and from Kenny Rogers. That was what made the sweep possible. You've got to catch the ball, and you've got to throw it. It all starts with pitching. We've been throwing the ball better lately, and consequently we've been giving ourselves a chance to win games.

This was a big game for Miguel Cabrera, too. He really smashed that home run to right, and in a pressure situation, which is something he hasn't been doing before this. Now we'll see if that home run does something for him the rest of the season. Only Cabrera knows what is happening with him mentally.

I can only speak from my own experience, but the thing about Cabrera that people who have never played this game don't understand is what happens to you, psychologically, when you sign a big contract. I don't care if it was 15 years ago or 20 years ago, when a million dollars was a big deal, or today when it's $152 million, players react differently when they sign big contracts like that.

I believe a lot of athletes are guilty of trying to do too much to prove they deserve the big money they're getting, regardless of how much it is. I have yet to see a player who gets a fat new contract and says, "OK, now that I've got the money, I don't have to play hard anymore." That just doesn't happen. You don't compete your whole life to get to this level and then all of a sudden throw in a white towel. It doesn't work that way. Instead of slacking off and mailing it in every day, players are often guilty of trying to do too much. I think that is what has happened to Cabrera since he signed that $152.3 million contract in spring training.

He's a 25-year-old kid who had been under the radar down in Florida. Now he's suddenly expected to do a lot. Everybody is pointing fingers at him. It's only natural that he would feel that pressure.

JUNE 13, 2008
DETROIT, MI
The Tigers resumed interleague play tonight with a 5–0 victory over the Los Angeles Dodgers. It was their fourth win in a row—matching their longest winning streak of the season—their sixth victory in their past seven games, and their first shutout of the season. This is the deepest the Tigers have gone into a season without shutting out somebody since 1996.

"We're having a little fun for a change," manager Jim Leyland said. "I think we're getting better. If we just go about our business, I think we'll be okay. I think everybody was pressing earlier. The guys were on edge a little bit. I think now we're starting to realize, 'Hey, we're a good baseball team.'"

The Tigers are now 28–3 when scoring five runs or more.

· · · ·

I understand it may be good for the game and good for the fans, and it may generate a little extra money, but I'm not a big proponent of interleague play. It's just not a fair schedule.

The only way to determine if you are the best team in your division or the best team in your league is if everybody plays everybody else an equal number of times. With interleague play, one team might get a pass for a weekend. They might end up playing a team from the other league that has had a rash of injuries or might be a bad team, while their rival in their division has to play a team from the other league that is red-hot. One team steals three wins while their rival gets swept, and those games all count the same in the standings.

There is no way every team in the American League can play every team in the National League an equal number of times every year, so somebody is always going to get an advantage. And that can affect which team wins in a division. That's the only reason I'm against interleague play.

I think the novelty has worn off a little bit. Unless we're going to start playing everybody in the other league, I don't really see the sense in it.

JUNE 15, 2008
SAN FRANCISCO, CA

After completing their successful homestand with a 5–4 victory over the Los Angeles Dodgers at Comerica Park this afternoon, the Tigers flew to San Francisco aboard *Tiger One*, the DC 9 owned by Mike Ilitch that serves both the Tigers and Ilitch's Stanley Cup–champion Detroit Red Wings.

Having their own team plane allows the Tigers to travel in style and avoid the hassles of security lines at the airports, lost luggage, and delayed or canceled flights—things that regularly haunt the average traveler.

·   ·   ·   ·

Obviously, tonight, the plane ride was good. When you sweep the White Sox and then you sweep the Dodgers in consecutive series, it does a lot for your team psychologically.

We swept New York at the end of April, and everybody thought we were finally on a roll then. But we went into Minnesota and wet the bed. So it was big for us to keep it going this time.

I said before we started the series against Chicago that it was imperative that we win at least two out of three, and we got three out of three. Having said that, to keep it going and accomplish another sweep in the fashion that we did was really big.

We played good defense on this homestand, we got good pitching, and we scored enough runs. I think part of our problem early in the year was that we fell into the trap of thinking, *Hey, with our offense, we can score any time we want*. That was everybody's feeling, even though we tried not to think that way. We fell into that trap of thinking we could just put it on autopilot and score eight or nine runs any time we wanted to. Well, this is the big leagues. That just doesn't happen up here.

We were beating ourselves an awful lot earlier in the year, and we haven't been doing that lately. Even though our pitching is still in the bottom half of the league, it's gotten a lot better. A lot better!

I ended up standing for most of the flight out to the West Coast tonight because my seat around the poker table has been taken by the manager, Jim Leyland. I was still in the game, I just had to stand. We play poker on every flight. Usually it's pitching coach Chuck Hernandez, hitting coach Lloyd McClendon, bullpen coach Jeff Jones, Jim Leyland, sometimes third-base coach Gene Lamont, and myself.

Of course, we play for money, and let's just say it has been a good year for me. My poker skills have become more refined this season than they were in years past. It's not just about the money, it's about the titles. It's about the bracelets, like they say in those big poker tournaments on TV. I've won so many bracelets this year that I've run out of room on my one arm and I'm about to go to my other arm. We don't actually give out bracelets in our games, of course, but I'm thinking about going to a jewelry store while we are in San Francisco and buying one.

The food on our flights is terrific. We get chicken or fish or steak. Coming out of Boston back in April, we had the best clam chowder I've ever had in my life. They have salads and fruit and chocolate-covered strawberries—just like the food you get on regular commercial flights. Yeah, sure.

There are a lot of advantages to having your own plane instead of flying charters or commercial flights.

We all have our assigned seats. We sit in the same seat on every flight. Every seat is a first-class seat, and some of them are facing each other around tables, so you're able to play cards. It gives the players a chance to build relationships.

You can watch movies, you can read, you can take a nap, or you can play cards. I'd say most of the guys are usually doing something that involves a deck of cards.

JUNE 17, 2008
SAN FRANCISCO, CA

Four months ago, it wasn't certain Marcus Thames would even have a place on the Tigers this season. Tonight, he made a place for himself in the Tigers record book.

Thames continued his home-run binge, clearing the outfield fence for the fifth game in a row with a mighty 465-foot blast, matching a feat accomplished by just four other Tiger sluggers—Rudy York (1937), Hank Greenberg (1940), Vic Wertz (1950), and Willie Horton (1969)—as the suddenly resurgent Tigers topped the Giants, 5–1.

Each of Thames' last eight hits has been a home run, a remarkable achievement in itself. And all eight have come off right-handed pitchers. Not bad for a guy who was supposedly going to platoon with Jacque Jones in left field this season and only play against left-handed pitchers.

Thames has hit eight home runs in his last 10 games, and the Tigers have won eight of those games.

"I may be dumb, but I'm not an idiot," manager Jim Leyland said. "He's won the left-field job, at least for now.

"Marcus is a two-run homer or a three-run homer waiting to happen. He's a threat every time he walks up to the plate. And he hits 'em when they mean something. This guy hits big ones. He may not hit 'em as often, but Marcus has as much home-run power as anybody in the American League. And when he hits 'em, they just keep going. No ballpark is going to hold 'em.

"He's a gentleman, he's a gamer, and he's a good teammate."

How big of a home-run threat is Marcus Thames? Consider this: In the last three years, ever since Jim Leyland—at the urging of his brother, Larry, who had watched Thames perform at Triple A Toledo—began trying to find a place for Marcus in the Tigers' lineup, Thames has homered once in every 12.88 at-bats.

To put that number into perspective, Barry Bonds, baseball's all-time home-run king at 762, hit a homer once every 12.92 tries. Ruth (714 HRs) cleared the fences once every 11.76 at-bats. Hank Aaron (755) averaged a home run once every 16.4 at-bats. Willie Mays (660) hit a home run every 16.5 at-bats. Mickey Mantle (536) hit a homer every 15.1 trips to the plate. Ted Williams (521) did so once in every 14.8 at-bats. Al Kaline, the Tigers' all-time home-run leader with 399, hit a homer once in every 25.4 at-bats.

After Thames latest blast, Larry Leyland left his brother a voice mail that said, "Do you believe me now?"

Two years ago, on Saturday, June 24, 2006, Larry Leyland's daughter, Courtney—Jim Leyland's niece—gave birth to a baby. And Marcus Thames hit a home run that day to tie the game against the St. Louis Cardinals, a game which the Tigers eventually won.

On June 7 of this year, Courtney delivered another baby. And, believe it or not, Thames belted another home run to tie another game, which the Tigers also won.

Manager Jim Leyland called Marcus Thames "a two-run homer waiting to happen." In 316 trips to the plate in 2008, Thames homered 25 times—once every 12.6 tries. "When it comes to pure power, Marcus actually has more power than Hank Aaron," said Andy Van Slyke.

This time the baby was a boy. "I don't know if they're going to name it Marcus," Leyland joked, "but I am going to tell her and her husband to get busy and have another one."

. . . .

That home run tonight was as majestic as any I've seen in a long, long time. Aesthetically and auditorily, it was really beautiful. It was beautiful both to my eyes and to my ears.

We were waiting for somebody to pick up our ballclub and carry it. Marcus Thames wasn't the guy we were expecting to do that, but he certainly has that capacity. I've said it time and time again: Marcus Thames has as much or more power than anybody in the game today. I'm talking about Ryan Howard and Albert Pujols and all of the other great hitters in the game.

Marcus just doesn't hit with as much consistency as those guys do. But for pure, raw power, Marcus Thames has as much or more than anybody.

When an athlete with that kind of an arsenal gets confidence, when he gets in that zone, there's no limit to what he can do.

I never saw Henry Aaron play in person, but Henry Aaron was what I call a wrist hitter. That's Marcus Thames. Marcus has tremendous wrists. In that respect, anyway, they're an awful lot alike. I'm certainly not comparing Marcus Thames to Henry Aaron, but Marcus is bigger than Aaron was and Marcus hits the ball farther than Aaron did.

When it comes to pure power, Marcus Thames actually has more power than Hank Aaron.

From my position on the field, in the first-base coach's box, I can usually tell how far a ball is going to go. Sound can dictate distance. And when Marcus hits a baseball, it makes a different sound than when 99.9 percent of the players in the game hit a ball. Marcus' hits sound different that Cabrera's or Magglio's or Guillen's do. Absolutely. It's sort of like being at a concert, when the music is pounding off your clothes. Marcus has that vibrating sound when he hits a ball.

If the average fan had the opportunity to stand behind the batting cage and listen to Marcus Thames hit the baseball versus, say, me hitting the ball, they would understand what I'm talking about.

Even at my age, at 47, I might be able to hit a ball down the line and get it out of the ballpark. But I guarantee you, even if somebody had their back turned to the batting cage when Marcus Thames hit a ball down the line and out of the ballpark, they could tell the difference between my home run and his. His home runs make a different *whack*. His home runs have about three more *A*s in them than mine. His home runs are like, *Whaaaack!*

JUNE 21, 2008
SAN DIEGO, CA
Marcus Thames continued his home-run rampage, belting No. 14 for the season, to propel the Tigers to a 7–5 victory over the Padres. Of Thames' last 10 hits, nine have cleared the fence or left the park.

"I'm seeing something I've never seen in my career," said veteran closer Todd Jones, who picked up his 13th save of the season and the 314th of his career, tying him with Robb Nen for 15th place all-time. "What Marcus Thames is doing is incredible."

Thames' home run may have thrilled his teammates and those Tigers fans who stayed up late to watch the game on TV back in Detroit, but Marcus was more exited about the autographed balls he received from Hall of Famers Willie Mays and Dave Winfield and former Brooklyn Dodgers pitching star Don Newcombe at a luncheon saluting the Negro Leagues earlier in the day.

"They came to me yesterday and asked if I'd be there," Thames said after tonight's game. "I was like, 'I'll be there two hours early.' It was awesome to meet those guys. I was like a little kid."

. . . .

Even though, until recently, Marcus rarely was in the lineup regularly, he is very popular in the clubhouse. His mother, Veterine, was paralyzed from the neck down in a car accident 25 years ago. Marcus lives with that every day. But unless somebody brings it up, he never mentions it.

I couldn't be happier for the guy. Marcus Thames has worked as hard as anybody I've ever seen or been around.

The thing most people don't realize is, Marcus works on his defense as much as he works on his hitting. As well as what he is doing offensively, he wants to be accountable defensively, which is really great to see. Marcus Thames has worked really hard on his defense, and he wants to continue to work at it. That's important.

When I first got here, I'll admit I was fearful of balls being hit to him. Now I look forward to him making plays, and he makes a lot of them.

The criticism against Marcus Thames has always been his defensive play in the outfield. Well, he's changed that.

I've worked with Marcus Thames a lot. A lot. The fact that he wants to work on his defense, the fact that he wants to improve his outfield play, is the most important part of elevating his play and becoming a consistently good outfielder.

Marcus is willing to work at what I call "game speed." My experience has taught me that you get to a high level of play by practicing at a high level. And to maintain that level, you need to continue to practice at a high level.

I can hit fly balls to you; I can hit fly balls to my 11-year-old son, Nathan; I can hit fly balls to Joe Six Pack who comes to the ballpark to watch the games; but I can't hit fly balls at game speed to anybody except a major-league outfielder and expect them to catch the ball.

By *game speed*, I mean I don't hit lazy, routine fly balls that almost anybody can catch. I can hit routine fly balls to my son, and he can catch them. But if I hit a line drive into the gap or a drive on which he has to make a shoestring catch, he ain't gonna make it because he's not physically capable of doing that yet.

But for a player like Marcus, if he is willing to practice at game speed, the game eventually slows down for him. And the game has slowed down, defensively, for Marcus Thames.

He tries to catch every ball in practice. He works on catching fly balls up against the wall. He crashes into the wall during our workouts. He throws the ball back in to me at game speed. He doesn't lob the ball back in to me. All those little things—I call 'em *reps* or *repetitions*—all those little things add up. And they make a difference in the actual game.

You might have to do a couple hundred reps before you're ready to make a play in the outfield. But when the time comes, and you make that play, you say to yourself, "All that work was well worth it because I helped my team win a ballgame with my defense." Believe me, as a former outfielder myself, I can tell you there's a lot of satisfaction in that.

Marcus is so much more comfortable going after balls now. He is taking better routes to get to the ball, he doesn't drop balls anymore, he doesn't take bad routes anymore, and he throws the ball better. I couldn't say that about him two years ago. Marcus makes a lot of nice plays now. I look forward to watching him play the outfield.

I'm happy for him. I'm not happy for myself as a coach for helping to make him a better player. That's my job. I'm no different than a hoe is for a gardener. A gardener can use a hoe or he can use his hands. I happen to think he is better off using a hoe. I'm just a tool for players like Marcus to use, players who want to get better.

The fact that Jim Leyland has decided to play Marcus against right-handed pitchers as well as left-handers makes a difference, too.

I'm a left-handed hitter, and, of course, Marcus bats right-handed. But I think there's a parallel there. When I played in St. Louis for the Cardinals, some people, including manager Whitey Herzog, didn't think I could hit lefties. Just as the "book" on Marcus Thames said he couldn't hit righties.

So, for a long time, I only played against right-handers. There were a couple of years when I led the National League in batting average against the top five starters in the league, all of whom happened to be right-handed pitchers.

But my premise about left-handed hitters has always been that playing against left-handed pitchers helps make them better hitters against right-handed pitchers. And the same is true of Marcus Thames batting against right-handed pitchers as well as against lefties.

As a left-handed hitter batting against a left-handed pitcher, you really have to focus on hitting the ball to center field and left-center. When you only face right-handed pitching as a left-handed hitter, you end up trying to pull too much, which lowers your average.

When I started playing every day for Jim Leyland in Pittsburgh, it really changed the way I approached right-handed pitching, and I became a more dangerous hitter.

I can see the same thing happening with Marcus Thames.

JUNE 26, 2008
DETROIT, MI

Within the space of 17 hours, Gary Sheffield won one game against the St. Louis Cardinals, 8–7, with a walk-off single and tied another the next day with a clutch ninth-inning home run that set up a 3–2 10-inning win when rookie Clete Thomas walked with the bases loaded for the second time in the game to force home the winning run.

In the three games since Sheffield returned from the disabled list, where he was recovering from a strained oblique muscle in his left side—an injury that may have turned out to be a blessing in disguise because it gave his surgically repaired right shoulder two uneventful weeks in which to heal—the 39-year-old designated hitter is batting .462 with two home runs.

"If I'm healthy, I know I'm one of the best in the game," said Sheffield matter-of-factly. "People don't realize how serious my [off-season] surgery was. That type of surgery is career-ending for pitchers. Hopefully now I can turn the corner, put that behind me, and be the hitter than I know I still am."

Asked what a healthy Gary Sheffield would mean to the Tigers, Jim Leyland summed it up in one elongated word: "Whooooo!"

This much is certain: Sheffield is swinging the bat better than he has at any time since he injured his shoulder in a freak outfield collision with Placido Polanco 11 months ago.

•　•　•　•

The fact is, Gary Sheffield, Kenny Rogers, Justin Verlander, Magglio Ordonez, Miguel Cabrera, all the guys that we were counting on to make us a very good team, have to at least have average years in order for us to have a chance to be competitive in September.

What has been going on with Gary Sheffield for these first three months is not really his fault. It's the result of the injuries he has suffered. Being 39, like he is, I think it's been harder for him to come back from those injuries than it was when he was, say, 29.

I think the severity of his surgery during the off-season took him by surprise. In spring training, he thought he was going to be ready. Instead, he took a couple of steps backward, physically. What we saw was a very frustrated, unhealthy Gary Sheffield at the plate. The results just weren't there.

But Gary's experience is going to start to show, provided he can play physically. He has always hit, and I think he's going to hit, but he's not going to hit if he's not healthy.

You could tell his shoulder was hurting him during the first three months. He didn't have bat speed. Gary, when he's healthy, has as violent a swing as anybody I've ever seen. And his swing just didn't have that same violence to it earlier this season.

He tried to overcome that lack of bat speed by cheating to get to the fastball. And when you cheat like that, when you're starting your swing early, you become more vulnerable to off-speed pitches.

Gary Sheffield is a great fastball hitter, and he's a good breaking-ball hitter. But when he's got to cheat to get to the fastball—which is something he has never had to do before in his career—it makes him vulnerable to breaking balls, which he was.

But if he's healthy now, he's going to be a big part of the story this year. Today, however, Clete Thomas was the story.

It's very unusual to see any game end with a walk. Games usually end with a base hit or a home run.

I was impressed with the fact that Clete didn't expand his strike zone in those two bases-loaded at-bats against the Cardinals. He didn't look like a rookie at the plate.

Nobody goes up to the plate thinking, *I'm going to get a walk*, unless you know you are completely overmatched. Especially not in the bottom of the tenth inning with the bases loaded and two outs. You're thinking, *I've got to get a hit*.

It's one thing to have the hitter in front of you walk. It's another thing to have the hitter in front of you walked intentionally. That was what happened to Thomas when the Cardinals intentionally walked Miguel Cabrera in the tenth inning this afternoon.

That puts added pressure on you as a hitter. You're thinking, *The opposing team, the opposing manager, in this case Tony La Russa, is telling me that I can't get the job done, because he's walking the other guy to pitch to me*.

That makes you even more anxious as a hitter. It really does. You want to show the other team and the other manager that you can swing the bat. I think that's true of anybody, especially with two outs, in a tie game, in extra innings. That at-bat had all of those ingredients.

The fact that Thomas was able to hold back and not swing on those last two pitches, a change-up and a fastball, after he fouled off a pretty good pitch at 2–2 to stay alive, really showed me something.

When you've got a young guy like Clete Thomas up there, who has not been in that position before, you don't know how he's going to react.

Obviously, he reacted in the correct manner. I think that will pay dividends for him, especially if he finds himself in that same situation again later this year.

Most of my conversations with Clete Thomas have focused on the mental aspects of the game: What I see in him, what I think he can do, and what he should expect. Things like that.

He works at his defense quite a bit. The fact that he can really run and really, really throw is going to be an asset for him for many years to come.

He's a hard-nosed player. I watch him slide into second base. Even when he's out, he makes good contact with the second baseman. He does everything he can to break up a double play. That's a good sign. His willingness to do that may win a ballgame for us someday. Who knows, we may end up winning the pennant by one game.

I like it when we have a combination of older veterans and some young players in the lineup. Guys like Clete Thomas bring energy and excitement to the game. I like that.

JUNE 28, 2008
DETROIT, MI

After blowing a three-run lead with two outs to go in the game and with ace closer Todd Jones on the mound, the Tigers rallied for a wild, dramatic 7–6 bottom-of-the-ninth win over the Colorado Rockies as Miguel Cabrera came through with his biggest hit yet as a Tiger, a clutch, two-run double that catapulted his team to the .500 plateau for the first time this year.

The Tigers have now won 16 and lost four since June 7 when their overdue about-face began.

"We're better off than we were three weeks ago, let's put it that way," said Jim Leyland who declined, as usual, to go overboard.

· · · ·

Tonight I witnessed the best scene I've seen since I've been here—and that includes 2006, when we won the pennant. It was awesome. And I'm not talking about Miguel Cabrera's game-winning hit, either.

Cabrera rounded second base and ran toward third. The fans were screaming and the whole team was out there on the field going crazy, trying to mob him. But Cabrera just kind of ran through them. He ran straight off the field down into the dugout. Even though he had gotten the hit that won the game, he was the first guy into the dugout, and I was the second guy in. I was right behind him.

He keep right on running through the little hall behind the dugout and then up to the steps toward our clubhouse. There are a lot of steps, and they're kind of steep and there is a little landing, like a platform, halfway up between the two flights of stairs.

As Cabrera was running up that first flight of stairs, Brandon Inge, who is on the disabled list and who had been in the clubhouse during the game taking treatment on his pulled muscle, came screaming out of the locker room, running down the top flight of stairs.

I guess Brandon must have been in the shower when Cabrera got the hit because he came running down the steps stark naked and soaking wet!

When they both got to that little landing in the middle, Brandon leaped into Miguel's arms like a little kid.

There were the two biggest kids on our team—Inge and Cabrera—one completely naked with water from his shower still dripping off him in the arms of the other, who just got the game-winning hit. It truly was a picture worth a thousand words.

Then Cabrera carried Inge, wet and naked, in his arms up the whole second flight of stairs and into the clubhouse.

Chapter 6

JULY

"On the Back Nine and Running Out of Holes"

JULY 2, 2008
MINNEAPOLIS, MN

The Tigers were shut out today, 7–0, by the Minnesota Twins—the 10th time their so-called Murderers' Row lineup has been blanked this season. It marked the first time the recently resurgent Tigers dropped two games in a row since early June. The Tigers are now 0–13 when they muster five hits or fewer and 4–38 when scoring four runs or less.

"I know anything is possible, but with our lineup you wouldn't think that could happen," admitted Brandon Inge.

. . . .

The Twins have built this team, and they have built Twins teams in the past, to fit their ballpark. You've got to give them credit for that. They know what they're doing. They're a good team.

Other teams coming in here to the Metrodome to play know the Twins having Joe Nathan at the back end of their bullpen shortens the game. Psychologically, that has an affect. You know you've got to score early.

But the one thing that impresses me more than anything about the Minnesota Twins—and I don't know why it is; I don't know whether it starts in the minor leagues or wherever—is it seems like every year the Twins walk the fewest batters in baseball. Their pitchers aren't afraid to throw the ball in the strike zone. They pitch to contact.

It's a philosophy that has always worked well for them, especially when you come in here to the Metrodome to play.

Personally, I really do not like coming to this ballpark at all. The Metrodome is the most unique place in the American League to play. And, in a lot of ways, it is also the most annoying place to play.

Aesthetically, it certainly is the ugliest. This ballpark just has a murkiness to it. There is no cleanliness, no crispness to the Metrodome. The noise is deafening, they've got artificial turf, and you're playing inside. It smells—believe me, it smells terrible in the visitors' dugout. That may be from all of the teams that have gotten their brains beaten in here over the years and all of the carnage that has been left in the visitors' dugout.

Whatever the reason, this really is a strange place.

You can hardly see the fans from the field during the game because they are so high up, so far away from you. And it's really noisy in here because, with the dome, the noise has no place to go. I have never been here when it was totally full, like during the playoffs or the World Series, but I'm sure the noise can be deafening. Or it can be music to your ears if you're a Minnesota Twin.

JULY 6, 2008
SEATTLE, WA

It took four hours and 12 minutes to complete, and a total of 458 pitches were thrown by the two sides this afternoon, but the Tigers finally edged the Mariners, 2–1, thanks to Miguel Cabrera's fifteenth-inning double and Marcus Thames' sacrifice fly off third-string Seattle catcher Jamie Burke, who was called upon to fill in when the Mariners ran out of relief pitchers.

"I believe that is officially the weirdest game I've ever played," declared closer Todd Jones, who picked up his 16th save in what was only the Tigers' second win in 31 games this season in which they have scored two runs or fewer.

"That was one of our most satisfying wins after it was over because it was one of the most f*cking boring games I've ever been involved in," manager Jim Leyland said.

"I'd rather watch the Perrysburg [Ohio] water tower rust."

· · · ·

We got 'em right where we wanted 'em today. They had to go get their third-string catcher to pitch the last inning.

We can laugh about it now, but I really believe that if we hadn't scored that run off their catcher, Jamie Burke, who was pitching in the fifteenth, we probably would have lost this game.

After playing for so long, by the fifteenth inning both teams were looking for any kind of an emotional lift. Both teams needed a little burst.

Basically, for more than nine innings, the game was really boring. Every inning looked the same as the last one and the next one.

When Burke came into the game, the fans finally came alive. The players on both sides came alive. It was something different, seeing a catcher take the mound.

The worst part of being in that situation was that nobody on our team wanted to be the one to make an out against him.

The good news is, we scored a run. But we might not have even scored then if Burke hadn't thrown a wild pitch to put Michael Hollimon, who was pinch-running for Miguel Cabrera, on third.

It was really imperative that we score that inning. If we hadn't scored, it would have been a huge letdown and the Mariners would have gotten a big lift. They would have felt like they had gotten away with something, sending a catcher out to pitch.

I tried to pitch once, myself, when I was playing for the Pirates, but Jim Leyland, who was my manager, wouldn't let me do it. We were in an extra-inning game and we ran out of pitchers, so I went to Jim and said, "Let me pitch. I can get these guys out."

But he wouldn't do it. Jim said he thought it was more important to keep his job than it was to win that one game. I guess Jim figured if I had hurt my arm pitching, he would have gotten fired.

I said earlier in the year that our goal was to get back to .500. Today's win put us there again. Now our goal is to get everybody healthy and keep winning consistently.

If Magglio Ordonez, Miguel Cabrera, Curtis Granderson, Carlos Guillen, and Placido Polanco don't play at their highest level, we're not going to win. Period. They just have to play at that level; there is no other answer.

Our pitching has had a good month, and our bullpen seems to be getting better. The elements are there.

Maybe Chicago really is as good as they've looked, but I cannot see them playing like that for the rest of the year. They really haven't been hit yet by the injury bug that hit us, and they're an old team in some ways. Can they maintain that? I don't know. We're going to find out, and they're going to find out.

But right now, I don't think we can be worrying about the White Sox or the Twins. Right now, we've got to worry about us doing what we can do.

JULY 12, 2008
DETROIT, MI

Three critical games against Central Division rival Minnesota, three agonizing one-run losses—the latest, 6–5, despite two-run homers from rookie Matt Joyce and Curtis Granderson this afternoon—left the Tigers 6½ games behind the opportunistic, second-place Twins and 7½ games removed from first place.

"If these games don't hurt, you should go home," Jim Leyland growled. "I hope the guys out there [in the locker room] are hurting as much as I am. If you don't hurt in your stomach after games like this, you should pack up your bags and go home.

"They [the Twins] are doing just enough—and we're just not doing enough. It's as simple as that."

.   .   .   .

I had a theory after we won that 15-inning game in Seattle that we could put that in a compartment in our brains, and the next time we were involved in a situation like that, in another extra-inning game, we could pull that win out and realize what it takes to grind out a win in extra innings. I really thought that game would have a long-term, positive effect on us. Like, we've done it once, so we can do it again.

To play that long, to grind that hard, and to pull the game out at the end of the day can be very uplifting. At this point in the season, that kind of a lift is at a premium.

But in the first game of this big-game series at home against the Minnesota Twins on Thursday afternoon, my theory went right out the window.

We had a 6–2 lead on the Twins in the fourth inning in the opener. We had emotion and momentum on our side. At least we should have had momentum after winning the first two games on this homestand against Cleveland. We had won 22 of our last 30 at that point, and it looked like things were finally coming together. We finally looked like the team we felt we were in spring training. I was thinking, *OK, if we win this game, we can almost catch the Twins before the All-Star break.*

Forget about Chicago. We've got to climb ahead of Minnesota and take over second place before we can start worrying about first place. So when we got up 6–2 in the fourth inning on Thursday, I was thinking, *OK, now we're going to make our move.*

But we lost that first game, 7–6, in 11 innings, because our bullpen let the lead get away again. And then we also lost the last two nights, also by one run in each game.

That's three one-run losses in a row. In our situation, that is extremely tough to take. Extremely tough. It's really hard to describe how mentally devastating something like that can be.

To be that close in every game, to be breathing down the Twins' necks, and to lose all three games by one run—that was awful.

In the second game, which we lost 3–2, the Twins made four great plays against us defensively. If those balls had been a foot more to the right or a foot more to the left, we would have had four more hits, we would have won the game, and everybody would have been thinking, *Isn't it great how we bounced back after that loss?*

With one swing of the bat, one base hit in a particular situation, we could have won any one of these last three games. With three of those swings we could have easily won all three. It's really that simple. Instead, we lost all three.

It just goes to show you, the Minnesota Twins are not flukes.

When you say "Minnesota," it doesn't carry the same weight as when you say "Boston" or "New York," but the fact is, the Twins have a lot of talent on that team. They're not names that make you start to shake, but when you look at that lineup before the first pitch is thrown, you see they've got a lot of good hitters on that ballclub. They play good defense, their pitchers aren't afraid to throw strikes, and they've got guys who can run like the wind.

I know it's a cliché, but speed never, ever, goes into a slump—unless a guy pulls a hamstring.

I'm sorry, but when you've got players like that, you've got yourself a good ballclub that's hard to beat. The Twins have got a lot of weapons.

The Twins can win games with their offense. As we just saw, they've got guys who can win games with one swing of their bats. Minnesota can win games on the base paths. Minnesota can win games with Joe Nathan coming out of the bullpen.

A lot of people don't realize Nathan is 26-for-26 in save situations against the Tigers. He has never blown a save in his life against us. We certainly don't get a good feeling when we see him coming into the game in the ninth inning. With him out there in the Twins' bullpen, it's automatically an eight-inning game for us.

If we were eight games over .500, we might have won all three of these games against Minnesota this weekend. But, being a .500 ballclub, there's always something that's a little short. It is a lack of clutch hitting, or it's a hanging breaking ball by one of our pitchers, or it's a routine ground ball that gets thrown away. It's always something.

It's always a little tiny thing that a .500 ballclub does that gets them beat. It's never that you're hitting 60 points lower than the other team. It's never that your pitchers' ERA is three runs higher. If that was the case, you wouldn't be a .500 ballclub. You'd be really bad.

But when you are a .500 ballclub, it's always one little thing or another that causes you to end up losing the ballgame. It's always a little tiny thing, and it always shows up when you play a big series. Those weaknesses always show up at the worst possible times.That's the difference between being a .500 ballclub and a team that is playing .600 ball, and that is what has happened to us all year.

As far as I can tell, these guys prepare properly for every game. They want to win. The desire is there. For whatever reason, we just haven't been able to put it all together.

And it's usually the little things.

JULY 13, 2008
DETROIT, MI
Rookies Clete Thomas and Matt Joyce belted home runs this afternoon to send the Tigers into the All-Star break feeling a little bit better about themselves, thanks to a sweep-saving 4–2 win over the Twins.

"It don't mean were gonna win the pennant," Jim Leyland cautioned. "But in the situation we're in, we need all the wins we can get.

"I'm telling you the cold, hard facts; I really believe we've got a chance," Leyland declared. "I really, sincerely believe we've got a chance.

"Is our chance as good as the White Sox's? No. We have to play exceptionally well, and they [the Twins and the White Sox] have to play not as well.

"But," Leyland added, "that's possible."

Comerica Park was sold out again today, the 19th time that has happened this season and the 16th game in a row in which the hometown crowd has topped 40,000.

For the first time this weekend, those folks went home happy today.

· · · ·

If we didn't win today, it would have been devastating.

OK, so now we're seven games behind the White Sox at the break, but we can't start worrying about that. If we are three games behind or four games back when we get to September, and we're still chasing the White Sox, then we can start scoreboard-watching. But not now; not yet.

Before we start thinking about stuff like that, we've got to figure out a way to get the two-out hit. We've got to figure out a way not to throw the ball away with a runner on third. We've got to figure those things out. We've got to worry about playing our game to the highest level that we can.

I don't think Chicago has ever mattered to us. The only time the White Sox matter is when they're out here on the field, right in front of us.

We're seven games back with 68 to play, but we can't afford to give in. The hardest part of this game is not giving in mentally. The average fan, I'd say 99 percent of the fans and most of the media, don't understand how mentally tough it is not to give in.

It's really hard to be at a high level mentally on every pitch. Believe me, it's really, really hard. And it's even harder when you're seven games away, the way we are.

It's a lot easier when you're out in front by 12 games. Two years ago, in 2006, it was easy. Everybody was having a good year. Everything was working. Every time you stepped up to the plate, you expected things to go your way.

When you're in the situation we've gotten ourselves into this year, you have to fight all the time to keep from wondering, *When is the other shoe going to fall?* That's the nature of the beast. It's the nature of the game. It's the proverbial little devil sitting on your shoulder saying, *Uh-oh, here you go again. Trouble is just around the corner. Something bad is going to happen. Be ready.*

When you are 10 games above .500, you don't have that little devil on your shoulder.

JULY 14–16, 2008

Baseball's All-Star break was better for some of the Tigers than it was for others.

Gary Sheffield spent the time vacationing in the Bahamas. Todd Jones went sightseeing with his family in Washington, D.C. Jim Leyland, one of the American League coaches for Tuesday night's All-Star Game, which was won by the AL, 4–3, in 15 innings, was George W. Bush's dinner guest at the White

Andy Van Slyke spent part of the All-Star break in the dentist's chair having his implanted two front teeth, which had been damaged, temporarily removed, leaving him with a gaping hole in the middle of his grin for the remainder of the season.

House on Wednesday. Carlos Guillen, the Tigers' lone All-Star this year after the team sent five to last summer's gala in San Francisco, got a hit and just missed a walk-off home run in the last All-Star Game that will ever be played in old Yankee Stadium.

Meanwhile, Andy Van Slyke went home to St. Louis, where his dentist removed his two front implanted teeth, leaving him with a gaping hole in the middle of his grin.

.   .   .   .

I'm really happy for Carlos Guillen; he deserved it. He is one of the smartest, hardest-working players I've ever been around.

The first time you go to the All-Star Game, it really is a big deal. It was an especially big deal for me the first time I went, which was in 1988 with Pittsburgh, where I finally got a chance to play regularly for Jim Leyland. If I had stayed in St. Louis under Whitey Herzog, I probably would never have been an All-Star, because Whitey didn't believe I was good enough to play every day.

But I got that opportunity in Pittsburgh. I made the All-Star team again in 1992, and I was picked the following year too, but I couldn't play because I had broken my collarbone.

I think, if people were honest, most of the players would admit that after they make the All-Star team once, they'd rather have the three days off.

Major League Baseball has tried to make the All-Star Game sound more important than it actually is by attaching the home-field advantage in the World Series to it. But the truth is, the All-Star Game doesn't mean much any more. It's really meaningless.

If your team is in a pennant race, having those three days off is more beneficial. It's more beneficial to you and more beneficial to your team.

The All-Star Game has changed so much for the players. It used to be important, I guess, many years ago, because as a professional player, it gave you an opportunity to compare yourself against the best players in the opposite league.

Back before there was ESPN, before we had interleague play and all of the games on cable television every night, you didn't get a chance to see the players in the other league much. The only chance you got to see a guy like, say, Reggie Jackson, play, especially in his early years, was during the All-Star Game and the World Series. You didn't even have video of the other teams' games to study in the clubhouse the way we do now.

So guys were constantly wondering whether they were as good as somebody in the other league. I think that made players cherish the chance to go to the All-Star Game much more so than they do today. I know it did for me, even in the late 1980s and early '90s.

The competitive nature of the All-Star Game has changed, too. You will never again see another collision at home plate in the All-Star Game like the one in 1970 when Pete Rose ran into Ray Fosse. No player would take a risk like that in the All-Star Game today. Back then the players in each league wanted to prove they were better than the players in the other league. They wanted to prove they were tougher. And for many years, the National League dominated the American League. Now that trend has reversed its course, and it's the American League that seems to come out on top every year. But it's not the same.

Back in 1970 what Pete Rose did wasn't even considered a dirty play. That was just the way the game was played then. But in 2008 if a player did what Rose did in that 1970 All-Star Game, he would be banished, at least in people's minds.

I guess that was kind of an ironic choice of words on my part, wasn't it?

JULY 17, 2008
BALTIMORE, MD

Before tonight's game, Jim Leyland challenged the Tigers to show how much this season means to them. "I'm not going to get into wins or losses, but it should mean enough to us to bust our butts for 68 games," he declared.

"Let's find out," the manager said. "Then, whatever happens, happens."

The players responded with a 6–5 win over Baltimore, thanks to home runs by Gary Sheffield, Brandon Inge, and Marcus Thames, and several sterling defensive plays by Inge, Miguel Cabrera, and even closer Todd Jones.

"That might be the luckiest, best play I've ever made," said Jones, who gloved Adam Jones' ninth-inning sacrifice bunt, whirled, and hurriedly threw to first base.

"That play was the Eighth Wonder of the World," Leyland declared.

"Todd never made a play like that before in his life, and he never will again.

"Nine times out of 10, on a play like that, Todd would have fallen down fielding the ball," Leyland added with a grin.

"And on the 10th time he would have thrown the ball to somebody in the mezzanine section."

.   .   .   .

The All-Star break can do funny things to a team sometimes. It can cement the feeling in the players' minds that, *Hey, we're not very good.*

When you've got three days off in a row like that, three days to do nothing but sit around and relax and take stock of things, you sometimes look at the teams ahead of you in the standings, and you wonder, *What are we really playing for at this point?*

I don't want to say teams quit, but a lot of clubs come back after the break realizing there is no hope for them at the end of the tunnel.

When you are busy, when you are caught up in the routine of the season, going to the ballpark every day, playing games every day, you don't always have time to stop and look at the bigger picture. Before you know it, you're six, eight, 10 games out of first place. When you're playing every day, those are just numbers, but when you've got three days off with no games and no batting practice, there is a reality check. You start to think about what those numbers mean.

Believe me, that is something that takes place over the All-Star break with a lot of players on a lot of clubs. They look at themselves and they say, *We ain't gonna make it.*

Well, let me tell you, we did not have that feeling on this club, coming back off the All-Star break tonight. We definitely did not. I know Jim Leyland certainly doesn't believe that. I know that we, as coaches, don't believe that. And the most important part is, the players on this team don't believe it, either. I sense there is a quiet confidence in our clubhouse, in our dugout, and on the field that this season is not over yet. I think we showed that against the Orioles tonight.

This was also the team's first chance to see me without my two front teeth. Actually, the guys love it. Before the game, I told both Edgar Renteria and Miguel Cabrera, "If you get to first base tonight, I promise I'll take my temporary bridge out and smile for you."

I'm certainly not suggesting that made either of them want to get to first base. It didn't, but it made them both laugh. Sometimes just a little thing like that can help a player relax, especially when you're in a situation like the one we're in right now.

As for my teeth, the post holding one of them in place broke and the area around the other became infected. The dentist opened up the whole area, scooped all the goop out, and gave me a temporary bridge. Nice All-Star break.

I have an appointment to have two new teeth on two news posts installed when I go back home on our off-day on September 11. That date is kind of apropos for me, I guess.

Until then, I can scare everybody every time I take out my teeth.

JULY 19, 2008
BALTIMORE, MD

The Tigers treated Nate Robertson to six first-inning runs tonight, but the left-hander couldn't hold the lead, exiting after just seven outs.

After battling back to reclaim the lead, the Tigers got caught up in a late-inning horror show. Baltimore's Ramon Hernandez homered off Joel Zumaya in the bottom of the ninth to tie the score; Placido Polanco scored the apparent go-ahead run in the top of the tenth only to be called out by plate umpire Brian Runge; and Luke Scott won the game with a walk-off home run off Freddy Dolsi in the bottom of the tenth, giving the Orioles an 11–10 win, and then added insult to injury by sliding into home plate.

. . . .

We are 0–2 this season when we score six runs in the first inning. That is unbelievable. Statistically, that is an anomaly. There is probably no other team in baseball that has scored six runs in the first inning twice this year and lost both games. There may not be another team that has done it once, and we've done it twice.

This was a tough game to lose. It was especially hard, losing like that after Placido Polanco was clearly safe when he slid into home on Gary Sheffield's single in the tenth inning.

I'll tell you something: I'll bet that particular play gets called wrong 50 percent of the time. Half of the calls on plays at home plate are wrong. I don't know why that is. I don't know if the umpires are out of position, I don't know if they're watching the tag rather than the player's foot, or what. A lot of times the throw beats the runner, but the catcher doesn't get the tag down in time.

But once a player's foot touches the plate, once his foot crosses that plane, I'm sorry, but he's safe. I don't even think a player's foot has to touch the plate. His foot just has to cross that plane.

I didn't see it, but I was told after the game that Luke Scott slid into home plate after he hit the game-winning home run for the Orioles in the bottom of the tenth. I know that as a player, if I was a pitcher and I ever saw somebody do something like that against my team, the next day I would tell that guy, "So, you like getting your pants dirty? Well, the next time you come up against me, I'm going to see to it that you do get your pants dirty again. Because you're going down."

I don't believe there was any malice on Luke Scott's part; I think it was just ignorance. But there is a lot less professionalism in the game today than there used to be. You can celebrate and have fun, but don't do it at the expense of your opponent.

The only solace in the whole situation is the fact that the White Sox ended up losing tonight, too. So we don't lose any ground. But we didn't gain any either, when we could have and should have.

At this point in the season we're like a golfer who is trailing in a tournament. If the leader makes a bogey and the golfer who is behind makes a bogey, too, he may go, "So what?" Well, it's not, "So what?" When the leader makes a bogey, you have to make a birdie or at least a par to try to catch up. That is the situation we're in. We're on the back nine at this point, and we're running out of holes.

We're looking for the leader to have a meltdown.

JULY 20, 2008
BALTIMORE, MD

With Jeremy Bonderman lost for the season and Dontrelle Willis sidelined indefinitely, it is up to Justin Verlander to bear an even bigger part of the pitching burden. Today he did exactly that, giving the weary bullpen a much-needed rest with 8⅔ strong innings in 96-degree heat, retiring 16 Orioles in a row at one point, to give the Tigers a 5–1 win and a split of their four-game weekend series against the Birds.

"That was a big-time pitcher coming up big-time for us when we needed it most," raved Jim Leyland in praise of his ace, who, for the third time in his last four starts, was called upon to halt a two-game losing streak. "That was an unbelievable effort. Tremendous. Absolutely tremendous."

Home runs by Magglio Ordonez and Marcus Thames gave the Tigers a total of 12 homers in their last six games.

Brandon Inge helped save the day with a highlight-reel stop on Kevin Millar's smash down the third-base line with two on and two out in the ninth.

"I remember thinking when the ball was hit, *There's no chance I'm going to let this ball get to the outfield,*" Inge explained later. "I was going to stop that ball, 100 percent. When I got my glove on it, I thought to myself, *Get rid of it as quickly as you can.*"

As stunned first baseman Miguel Cabrera gloved Inge's throw from his knees for the final out, Tigers coach Rafael Belliard began immediately mimicking the ESPN SportsCenter theme song in the dugout .

. . . .

My assessment of this season can be summed up in one word: *almost*. It has been an *almost* year for us, so far. We almost took three out of four from Baltimore. We should have taken three out of four from Baltimore, and we almost did.

We've had a lot of those *almost* moments this year. One night, it's we *almost* knocked a run in. The next game, it's we *almost* made the right pitch. But it is the teams that don't have the word *almost* in their vocabulary that end up playing in October.

It was a really great effort today. I think you could call this a *statement* game, the way we stepped up. We showed we're not out of this thing yet.

We split the four games against Baltimore. But if we had won three out of the four, like we should have, we'd feel a lot better about what's going on.

JULY 25, 2008
DETROIT, MI

The Tigers watched in horror in the ninth inning tonight as Jermaine Dye's two-out, two-run homer off Todd Jones sailed over Magglio Ordonez's head and into the right-center-field seats to suddenly turn an apparent victory into an anguishing 6–5 defeat.

The jubilation in the White Sox dugout as Dye rounded the bases said as much about the importance of this game and this three-game weekend series to both teams as the pained expression on the Tigers' faces as they walked off the field.

"You've got to get 27 outs, and we didn't do it," Jim Leyland acknowledged. "We had our opportunities to break the game open, and we didn't do it. We played hard. We just didn't play good enough."

"We're in a little bit of a pickle now," admitted Jones, who got the first two outs in the ninth before giving up a single to Chicago's Carlos Quentin on an 0–2 pitch and serving up the home run to Dye. "We're in a hole.

"What I do is pass/fail," Jones added. "Tonight, I failed."

. . . .

We wanted to give Chicago something to think about in this series. Absolutely. Where we're at right now, we're looking up at their behinds, we're chasing 'em. And we've got to get within reach before we can give 'em a little nudge just to let 'em know we're there. That is what this series is all about for us. But to do that, we've got to beat them first.

A lot of criticism will come down on Todd Jones for what happened tonight. He made some bad pitches, but that's part of the game.

He had Carlos Quentin 0-and-2, and he gave up too much of the plate, and Quentin got a base hit. Then he fell behind 2-and-0 to Jermaine Dye, who is a dangerous hitter, and he threw the ball up and over the plate. It was not a good pitch.

Nobody will ever be able to convince me, when a guy hits a ball out of the ballpark, that it was a good pitch. No good pitch ever leaves the ballpark. That can't be. It may have started off as a good pitch, but it ended up in a bad location.

You can't tell me you had good location on a pitch when a ball gets located in the seats. That's bad location. That's a very bad part of the ballpark for a pitch to end up.

JULY 26, 2008
DETROIT, MI
The Tigers had their ace, Justin Verlander, on the mound, and a crowd of 45,280—the largest in Comerica Park's nine-year history—in the stands tonight. They got home runs from Gary Sheffield and Magglio Ordonez.

But an overly pumped-up Verlander suffered his poorest performance since April as, for the second night in a row, the Tigers fell just short, 7–6, to drop seven games behind front-running Chicago.

"He [Verlander] was totally out of whack from the first inning," Jim Leyland admitted. "He was way out of synch. I'm sure he took this as a big game, which I wish he wouldn't have. But he took that attitude out to the mound. He was way too pumped up. He was just throwing."

• • • •

This was another one of those *almost* games I was talking about. Last night's game was, too. We had our chances to win them both, we *almost* won them both, and instead we lost them both by one run.

During tonight's game, I was thinking about how one game affects the next one. If we had won last night's game, like we should have, it would have changed Justin

Verlander's whole attitude when he took the mound tonight. And it would have changed Chicago's whole attitude toward him, too. But all that changed when we lost the first game of this series

If we had won last night, Verlander would have been much more relaxed when he took the mound tonight. He wouldn't have felt like the pressure was all on him. He never looked like himself, right from the first pitch. He was totally out of synch. You don't brush a guy back on the first pitch of the ballgame, the way Verlander did tonight. That doesn't do you any good.

We'll never know what the outcome would have been, but I know that the circumstances would have been very different if we had won that first game—both for us and for the White Sox.

Verlander would have been more relaxed. He probably would have thrown more strikes. You're not going to get anything done when you've thrown more than 100 pitches and you're just in the fifth inning.

And the White Sox might have been pressing a little more tonight with us just 4½ games behind them instead of 6½ back. That's a big difference psychologically.

I don't know if it's harder to lose by one run than it is to lose by four or five. But I do know this game of baseball is a lot harder to play than people think. Everybody thinks that just because football players put on shoulder pads and helmets that football is a harder game than baseball. Physically, maybe it is—for a couple of hours, anyway. But the mental aspect of baseball never gets its due. And when you lose games like this, it can mean the season is over for a lot of teams. I don't think that's going to be the case with these guys.

No. 1, these guys are too talented. No. 2, I think they want to finish out this season in the best way possible. And No. 3, they've got a manager who won't let 'em quit. Jim Leyland doesn't have any quit in him. Jim's last breath will be exhaling smoke. Literally.

JULY 27, 2008
DETROIT, MI
On a day on which Jim Leyland named Fernando Rodney his new closer, replacing 40-year-old Todd Jones, who was the goat of Friday night's ninth-inning loss to Chicago, the Tigers' manager watched Joel Zumaya leave the game in the eighth inning with tightness and spasms in his right triceps and then watched Rodney throw an unacceptable 42 pitches to finish the game. The bullpen has become a huge problem.

After the game, which the Tigers won, 6–4, over the first-place White Sox to avert a total weekend wipeout, Jones fought back obvious tears in a futile effort to maintain his composure.

"I'm 40 years old, you knew this day had to come sometime," said the man who, with 319 career saves, currently ranks 14th in baseball history and is easily the Tigers' all-time saves leader with 235.

"This is about the Tigers, this is about Detroit, this isn't about me," said Jones, whose $7 million contract expires at the end of the season. "It's about winning games."

Although Jones is 4–1 with 18 saves this season, opposing hitters have batted .375 against him in 11 appearances since June 28, and he has blown three of his last seven save opportunities. In his last 9⅓ innings, Jones struck out just one enemy batter.

"We're not throwing Todd Jones under the bus," Leyland said, in explaining his decision. "The reason Todd Jones is not the closer right now is because the quality of his pitches and the location of his pitches was not good enough."

.   .   .   .

People may look at the decision to take Todd Jones out of the closer's role and say, "That was an unemotional decision." But it was not. It was a very emotional decision, and it was a very hard one to make. Jim Leyland is not going to make a decision like that without totally thinking it through. He's had to make decisions like that in the past, and he'll make them again in the future when he deems them necessary.

A manager always tries to make decisions based on what is best for the team. The same goes for the pitching coach and the rest of the coaches on the staff. We talk about things, we talk about players, we talk about personnel all the time.

There are a lot of reasons why you make a decision like that. With Jones, there have been some hints that he may be having trouble with his shoulder, but ultimately it doesn't come down to what the first-base coach thinks or what the third-base coach thinks; that is the manager's decision. Jim has never ducked that responsibility, and that's what has made him a great manager.

One of the hardest things, I think, for any manager, is dealing with the psyche and the sensitivity of their closer. Todd Jones is an extremely sensitive guy. In some ways that makes no sense, I know, given the success Todd has had, not only here with the Tigers but throughout his career. But as smart and as competitive as Todd has been as a relief pitcher and a closer since his first day in the big leagues, he's still a very sensitive, introspective guy. Those two things don't normally go hand-in-hand.

To have been able to accomplish what he has accomplished in that role, with the makeup he has, is amazing. Don't get me wrong, it's not a bad makeup; not at all. I love Todd Jones. Todd Jones is like a brother to me, but he is who he is.

JULY 28, 2008
CLEVELAND, OH

The high-octane Tigers, who were supposed to set a franchise record for runs scored, were inexplicably shut out tonight for the major-league-high 11th time, 5–0, by the last-place Cleveland Indians and Paul Byrd, who is 10–2 lifetime against them.

The loss also ended the Tigers' streak of nine consecutive games in which they had collected 10 or more hits—the longest such streak in more than 50 years of Tigers baseball. Tonight, they could manage just four.

As a result, Jim Leyland excused his players from taking batting practice tomorrow, suggesting they were drained, physically and emotionally, by the weekend battle with the White Sox. Leyland admitted his team looked, "tired...sluggish...blah."

After the game, Leyland addressed his team. "I told them they can't get caught up in the standings," he explained. "They've been through a lot."

.   .   .   .

Once again, we demonstrated that we have had a very Jekyll-and-Hyde offense this year. As many runs as we have scored, that doesn't tell the story. In a lot of ways we look healthy, but we've got what, for lack of a better word, I guess I would call a cancer—a hidden disease. We may look healthy on the outside with our lineup, but inside there is something else going on with our offense.

I like our offense. I think it's a good offense. We have the capacity to beat anybody in the league on any given night. We have the capacity to score 20 runs in a game. But for some unknown reason, we unfortunately also have the innate ability not to score any. That makes no sense, I know, but it's true.

You know something in there is wrong, but you don't known exactly what it is, and you don't know how to cure it. I think part of the explanation is our inability to play "small ball." We can't manufacture runs. It's really difficult for us to hit-and-run and steal bases because we just don't have that kind of speed.

Plus tonight we were facing Paul Byrd. A lot of our players haven't seen a pitcher with a windup like that since American Legion ball. But he's probably as smart as any pitcher in the American League. He has got to be in order to win with what he's got. He just has our number. And he's got a few other people's numbers, too.

JULY 30, 2008
CLEVELAND, OH

On the eve of the trade deadline, about two hours before tonight's game against the Indians, the Tigers surprised everybody by trading catcher and future Hall of Famer Pudge Rodriguez to the New York Yankees for former Tigers reliever Kyle Farnsworth in an effort to bolster their struggling bullpen.

With Jorge Posada out for the year, the Yankees desperately needed a veteran catcher who could hit and, more importantly, cope with the pressure of playing in New York.

And with closer Todd Jones headed for the disabled list, Fernando Rodney's reliability still very much in doubt, and Joel Zumaya clearly not yet ready for prime time, the Tigers needed another reliever.

The thought of playing Russian roulette with his bullpen for the rest of the year was not something Jim Leyland relished.

The Tigers had already decided that they were going to let the 36-year-old Rodriguez go at the end of the season anyway rather than pay him the $20 or $30 million that he is sure to demand for the next two or three years. Once that decision was reached, there was little reason to keep him around—especially if they could make a trade that might bolster their bullpen for a possible stretch run.

Rodriguez was batting .295, which was a big part of the reason the Yankees were willing to make the trade. But Pudge is no longer the difference-maker he once was.

Rodriguez, long a favorite of Tigers' owner Mike Ilitch, who in February 2004 went to the Detroit hospital where Pudge was undergoing his physical exam to personally woo the free agent, became the face of the Tigers' long-awaited renaissance. He brought instant credibility to a long-floundering franchise that had failed a near-record 119 times the previous summer.

But for that, Pudge was very well compensated. Rodriguez collected $45.7 million from the Tigers over the past four seasons plus four months—at a time when no other team in baseball, no other owner except Ilitch, was willing to offer him anywhere near that much money or guarantee him anything close to five years of security.

However, in recent weeks, Rodriguez had grown increasingly unhappy about Leyland's plan to divide the catching duties between Pudge and Brandon Inge—in part, to keep Rodriguez fresh and in part to determine whether Inge could be the Tigers' every-day catcher in 2009.

In 2005, along with disgruntled Dmitri Young, Rodriguez helped to undermine Alan Trammell within the Tigers' clubhouse. Leyland was well aware of that when he arrived in Detroit. And some close to the team sensed a danger that attitude could resurface.

With Pudge Rodriguez, it was always all about Pudge. What else would you expect from a man who once had a larger-than-life statue of himself erected in his yard?

. . . .

It was a great trade, a really great trade for us. Statistically speaking, we need a guy like Kyle Farnsworth in our bullpen right now. We need a guy who can come in and pitch anywhere from the sixth to the ninth inning.

Farnsworth has been pitching well lately for the Yankees, and he pitched well for Detroit in the past. I don't care who you are, pitching in the eighth or ninth innings in Detroit is a lot easier than pitching in the seventh or eighth innings in New York.

There had been some talk among the coaches and Jim Leyland about the situation. There was talk about possibly trading Pudge Rodriguez. There's always talk. There's talk about most players.

A manager goes to his coaches and to other people whose opinions he trusts and says, "Hey, who's not tradable on this team?" I'm sure that takes place on every team in baseball. And Pudge Rodriguez did not fall into that "untradeable" category—not in anybody's mind. So when the situation arose where we needed another reliever and the opportunity arose to get one, the manager and the general manager made the trade.

But let me say this about Pudge Rodriguez: he is, in so many ways, exactly what you want in a baseball player. His physical commitment, his enthusiasm, his effort, his desire to play, his desire to compete, his desire to do well—Pudge Rodriguez, to me, is a Hall of Famer who got everything out of his ability.

Most Hall of Famers do. You can look back at some guys and say, "Darryl Strawberry should have been a Hall of Famer." You could probably name 25 guys like that over the years—guys who did not get the most out of their abilities. But Pudge is one the guys who did, and I have the utmost respect for him for that reason.

So many people on the outside think this is an easy game because players like Pudge make it look easy. But I know how much it takes, mentally and physically, on a daily basis, to become a player of that caliber.

Of course, Pudge is not the same player he was 10 years ago. Who is? Nobody is. Barry Bonds is the only Hall of Famer I can think of who defied his age. But Pudge defied his age to some extent, too, and he still is defying his age. He's an amazing player.

Of course, he had an ego. I think all great players in Pudge's category come across as being selfish. Barry Bonds certainly did. Was it about Barry? Sure it was. Is it about Manny with Manny Ramirez? Sure it is.

Human nature being was it is, great ballplayers absorb all that adulation and they become something bigger than what they are. Their image in their own minds is a lot bigger than they really are. They get self-absorbed, and they have to keep feeding that self-absorption, over and over and over again. They have to feed that monster. And where they try to feed that monster, that thing I call self-pride, is on the field. That's what drives all great players; they all have it.

Ted Williams wanted to walk down the street and have people say, "There goes the greatest hitter who ever lived." Joe DiMaggio always wanted to be introduced as, "The greatest living Yankee."

Personally, that makes me want to puke. I don't define someone's existence based on whether they can hit a fastball or not. But having said that, it seems to me the common equation in all great players is their need to keep feeding that ego, that monster. That comes across as being selfish, and it absolutely is.

But within that selfishness, they do a lot of winning—a lot of winning—and winning is what this game is all about.

I will tell you that this past week, with the length of our games and the emotional commitment that our guys have made, has been about as tough a week as a team can have. Watching these guys try to get up every night after they get beat—it's been hard. The Chicago series was tough. We lost two out of three there—two tough losses—and then we came back and won the third game. That showed me something right there.

Then we came to Cleveland and had 13 innings tonight. Fortunately, we won, 14–12, although it took five hours and 33 minutes to play.

I just wish tonight's game—or should I say this morning's game—had come a day later on the 31st, so we could have started it in July and finished it on August 1. Then we could have said, "That game took a month to play," because it certainly felt like that.

This game showed again, that, as many issues as this team has had this year—offensively, pitching-wise, bullpen-wise—this ballclub has character. This ballclub doesn't quit. You have to give them that. There's no give-in. Not a bit.

I wish the people at home watching this game on TV—if anybody actually stayed up that late—or the people who read about it in the paper, could have seen the celebration in our clubhouse after the game. The energy those players showed at 1:30 in the morning, after playing baseball for 5½ hours or whatever, all the high-fiving and cheering was a really neat thing to see.

Scenes like that are what make the season and all the hard work everybody has put in worthwhile. Those kinds of emotions are what keep you going.

JULY 31, 2008
CLEVELAND, OH

The Tigers let another golden opportunity for victory slip away this afternoon as they fell, 9–4, to the Indians in a game that brought sharp words of criticism from Jim Leyland toward his ace pitcher, Justin Verlander.

Calling his starter's 114-pitch count "a big concern," Leyland didn't mince words about Verlander's fifth-inning performance, in which the right-hander, among other things, walked Cleveland's No. 9 hitter, Asdrubal Cabrera, who was batting .199, on a 3–2 breaking ball. "That's not acceptable," the manager growled.

"We played fine—we just didn't pitch well enough," he said. "I thought Verlander would wipe that lineup out. He has to figure some things out. To sum this game up, the fifth inning was disastrous."

With two-thirds of the season now behind them, the Tigers are 55–53, even though since June 7 they are 14 games over .500, which shows how bad their start to this season really was.

Assuming it will take at least 90 wins to win the American League Central, the Tigers will now have to go at least 35–19 during the final third of this season to have a chance.

They are currently on a pace to win 83 games, hardly what anyone expected when this season began.

·　·　·　·

We just hit another downdraft. For the second time in a row, Justin Verlander whiffed when we really needed him. Again, that is a part of this season that doesn't make sense to me. That shouldn't be happening with him, but he's still fermenting in his career. A lot of times, when a pitcher is young and still fermenting, you get more disappointment than you think you should.

I've said it all year—I wish I could stop saying it one of these days—but I firmly believe we're a better club than our record indicates. But that doesn't matter. It does not matter. The fact is, the best team doesn't always win. The team that plays the best, the team that executes the best, wins. Believe it or not, I still think there is time for this team to turn things around. Jim Leyland has certainly relayed the fact that he feels this team can win. Hopefully the players buy into it.

We haven't soared yet. We keep hitting these wind pockets that shoot us up there, and then we hit a downdraft, like tonight.

Chapter 7

AUGUST

"This Cannot Be Happening"

AUGUST 3, 2008
ST. PETERSBURG, FL
Today, an obviously fed-up Jim Leyland used words like "disgusted," "embarrassed," "ashamed," and "shocked" to sum up his feelings on his team and this season. And that was before the Tigers blew another chance at victory, falling to the Tampa Bay Rays, 6–5, in 10 innings.

In a 20-minute pregame harangue, Leyland served notice that major changes could be coming—both in the lineup and in the starting rotation—if some of the underachieving players don't start producing.

Leyland was addressing the media in his clubhouse office at Tropicana Field when he spoke, but his words were clearly meant for his players' ears.

164 | TIGERS CONFIDENTIAL

"I'm not making threats, but I'm tired of this," Leyland declared, following a lengthy meeting with Tigers president and general manager Dave Dombrowski, who is along on this road trip.

"Some people have got to do better or there are going to be some changes," Leyland promised. "Some guys have got to step it up. Step up their approach and step up their tenacity.

"What's going on right now is not good enough. If we have to change some things and play some kids down the stretch, we will."

Leyland didn't name names, but he was most likely referring to designated hitter Gary Sheffield (.230, nine homers, 31 RBIs), shortstop Edgar Renteria (.253, five homers 37 RBIs), and pitcher Nate Robertson (6–8, 6.06 ERA).

"I'm not going to keep putting people out there who aren't producing," Leyland warned. "I'm not mad at anybody, but there are some guys who need to step it up. It's that simple.

"Some things are just not acceptable. You can't keep playing people or handing pitchers the ball and getting nothing. If some people can't play the rest of the season all-out, I'll put somebody else in there who can."

The Tigers' last two losses to Tampa Bay, in which they failed to take advantage of nine walks on Friday night and then threw 200 pitches in eight innings on Saturday, apparently were the last straws.

"I've been disgusted the last two nights when I went back to the hotel," Leyland said. "We got our butts kicked. If you're not embarrassed by that, you should be.

"They [the players] can get mad at me until the cows come home, but I've got people on my butt," admitted Leyland, who may be feeling some pressure from above for the first time since he took over the Tigers in 2006. "Bosses get nervous when things aren't going well. If I was my boss, I'd be ticked off right now. And it has a trickle-down effect.

"If I don't produce, I'll get fired. If I have to tell some people, 'I'm taking you out of the lineup or out of the rotation,' that's what I'll do. I won't hesitate.

"We should be embarrassed, and I'm not sure enough of us are," an agitated Leyland continued. "It's been a disappointment since day one. I've been more than disappointed. I've been shocked by our performance. This is a better team than the way we have played.

"I'm ashamed," Leyland continued. "I think we're too good to be playing like this and pitching like this. Maybe I've got them overrated, I don't know.

"If people don't start stepping it up, if time after time after time they don't produce, you have to go in a different direction. It's like fishing. I'm not going to sit at the same f*cking lake for a month and never get a nibble. I'm going to try a different lake—or try some different bait.

"Sooner or later, whether you like it or not, you have to tell the players and you have to tell the media that so-and-so, so-and-so, and so-and-so are not producing," Leyland said.

"There'll be no bullshit. It'll be eyeball-to-eyeball. When a player comes in to ask why he's not playing, I'll say, 'Because you're not doing shit.'

"We've had some performances that have been terrible. Overall, it just hasn't been good enough. That's why we're where we're at. We haven't taken the bull by the horns.

"We've got to step it up if we want to be in the hunt. If you don't want to be in the hunt, go home. Take an early vacation. Start your winter early and come back next spring. I'll bring some kids up to play.

"As a player, you can either sit there and say, 'Oh, well, it's just not our year,' or you can say, 'We've got to step it up. We've got to strap it on. Let's go.'

"There is a difference between effort and production," Leyland said. "Hustle and effort should never be an issue. Playing hard should be a no-brainer.

"But at this level, the next step is production. All I can do is put your name in the lineup. The rest is up to you. It's up to you to produce. If you produce, you play. If you produce, you pitch. It's that simple."

All things considered—rookie Armando Galarraga's six shutout one-hit innings; home runs by Gary Sheffield, Curtis Granderson, and Miguel Cabrera; and the way the Tigers battled back after Tampa took the lead in the eighth inning—today may have been their most crushing setback of the season.

"Say whatever you want, write whatever you want, you saw the game," an angry Leyland snapped after the game.

"That's all I've got to say about it. See ya later."

In losing these three games in a row to the Rays, the Tigers went 4-for-30 with runners in scoring position and stranded 33 men on base. Today's loss knocked them back below .500 for the first time since July 19.

New closer Fernando Rodney, who replaced Bobby Seay in the bottom of the tenth after the Tigers had grabbed the lead in the top half of the inning on Cabrera's towering home run, walked the first batter he faced, drilled pinch-hitter Shawn Riggans in the upper chest, and walked B.J. Upton before surrendering a game-tying single to Carl Crawford and then walking Carlos Pena to force home the game-winner with two away.

Two innings earlier, new reliever Kyle Farnsworth, who was presented with a two-run lead when he arrived in the eighth, had served up home runs to Tampa's Eric Hinske and Upton, turning an apparent Tigers victory into a 4–3 Rays lead.

·   ·   ·   ·

First off, it didn't make any sense the way Kyle Farnsworth had been pitching for the Yankees that he should come into this game and give up two home runs like that.

Then after the way we battled back to take the lead, we really felt we should have won this game. We knew that Chicago had already lost this afternoon. This would have been a big win for us, a huge win.

When Miguel Cabrera hit that home run leading off the tenth, at that point I felt more confident that we were going to walk away with the win in this game than I have all year. I thought, *We've got this game!* But that's the way this season has gone. Like I said, it's been a continuation of *almosts*.

I agree completely with what Jim said before the game. This is a business where, while the guys are expected to give their best effort, you still have to make the best of the cards that are dealt; you have to play the cards in front of you. You can have the aces, but if you don't play your aces right, you still can lose the hand. A lot of guys haven't played their cards correctly this year.

To use another poker term, the flop has gone against them.

AUGUST 5, 2008
CHICAGO, IL

There seems to be no end to the Tigers' frustration. This is beginning to sound like a broken record: Another big lead blown. Another opportunity wasted. Another crushing defeat.

The blame lay squarely on the bullpen again tonight as the Tigers, still 0-for-August, threw away a five-run lead and a chance to gain valuable ground on Chicago. Instead they failed for the fifth game in a row, 10–8, despite a pair of two-run homers by Placido Polanco, when Joel Zumaya, the designated closer for the night, served up a three-run homer to the White Sox's Nick Swisher in the bottom of the fourteenth inning.

. . . .

As I watched Nick Swisher's home run go over the fence in the fourteenth inning, I said to myself, *This is statistically impossible, what has happened to us in the last five days.* I can't believe it. I've never seen anything like it in all the years I've been in baseball. This cannot be happening to us. It defies all logic or explanation.

I'll tell you what, if I just lobbed the ball up there at 60 miles an hour, that couldn't have happened. It just couldn't.

I'm not saying that Nick Swisher isn't capable of hitting home runs. What I am saying is, teams shouldn't be able to hit home runs off us to win game after game like that. They just shouldn't.

Even during batting practice, when the coaches are lobbing the ball over the plate and the hitters are all trying to hit it out of the park, it's amazing how many times the balls land on the warning track or fall just short of going over the fence.

So when you get into the game, with a guy throwing 97 or 98 miles an hour, with the fans all screaming and the game on the line, it should be a whole lot harder to hit home runs. And it is.

When Placido Polanco hit his second home run tonight, in the top of the fourteenth, I was smiling to myself and thinking, *Okay, we're in.*

I mean, how often does Placido Polanco hit two two-run homers in a game? When our No. 2 hitter, who normally doesn't hit home runs, hits two in the same game, you've got to believe, *We're gonna win this game.*

On the field, in the first-base coach's box in the four-teenth inning, I was thinking, *Well, finally, an extra-inning game is going to go in our favor.* And let me tell you, if we had won this game, like we should have, Chicago would have been thinking, *Hey, now we've got two teams to worry about: the Minnesota Twins and the Detroit Tigers.*

But Edgar Renteria made an error on what should have been the second out in the bottom of the fourteenth inning, and things started to unravel from there. I'm not blaming Edgar for what happened, but one thing I do know about this game is, when you give first-place clubs like Tampa Bay or Chicago an extra out, they will find a way to take advantage of it and beat you; they just will. That's why they're in first place and we're not.

Now I'm afraid, after tonight's game, the White Sox may feel like they've put us way, way back in their rearview mirror. And that's fine; I can certainly understand why they might think that.

However, I can tell you this club doesn't think that way. We believe there's still time. But time is our enemy right now; there's no question about that. But that's not to say every-thing can't fall into place for us during the last six weeks of the season.

I will say that, in a lot of ways, this is a ballclub people should be really proud of; it really is. I know our record isn't what everyone expected it to be. It isn't what we expected it to be. But these guys haven't quit—they didn't quit tonight, and they haven't quit all year. I think that's a testament to the fortitude that Jim Leyland, the coaches, and the players have. We all have it. We know things aren't going our way. We know some guys aren't playing at their highest levels. We know that, and they know that.

But when things aren't going your way, there's one thing that you can control, and that's your fortitude. Even though we have played well below our expectations and the city of Detroit's expectations, these players haven't ever given up their fortitude.

Since Jim Leyland had that tirade after the series against Cleveland back in April 2006 when he thought the players had mailed it in, I haven't seen any signs of surrender around here.

That is a credit to Jim Leyland and to the players on our team.

AUGUST 7, 2008
CHICAGO, IL

Magglio Ordonez, who still derives extra delight out of beating or doing well against his former team, the White Sox, drove home two runs tonight with a ninth-inning triple as the Tigers averted a sweep with an 8–3 win over Chicago in this otherwise heartbreaking series.

Ordonez and White Sox manager Ozzie Guillen have long since kissed and made up. But the hard feelings that erupted on both sides when Ordonez fled to the Tigers after being unable to get what he considered a fair contract offer in

Chicago after undergoing radical knee surgery in 2004 have not been completely forgotten.

Ordonez, at the time, referred to Guillen, his former teammate and manager, as "my enemy."

Guillen, who is far less reserved and soft-spoken than Ordonez, called Magglio "a piece of shit."

The anger and emotions were real.

"He played with the wrong guy," the ChiSox manager said back in 2005. "He was bad-mouthing my team. He was bad-mouthing my trainer. He was bad-mouthing my general manager. He was bad-mouthing my owner. He was bad-mouthing my organization.

"But when he said, 'Ozzie,' as soon as he named me, it was on."

· · · ·

We wanted to win two games in this series against the White Sox. We got one.

At least, by winning tonight, we're only 7½ behind. That sounds and feels a whole lot better than going home 9½ back. Of course, if we had swept this series, we would have only been 3½ games back. That's a huge difference, statistically and psychologically.

I'll tell you something: this has been about as painful a two-week period as I've ever been through in my entire baseball career. To see how we have lost games, to think about how close we could be in this pennant race, and to look at where we actually are really hurts.

That first game in this series when we lost on that home run by Nick Swisher is still embedded in my mind. That loss just changed the whole complexion of this series. If we had won that one, like we should have, maybe Justin Verlander would have gone out and pitched a more relaxed game the next night and we would have won that one, too. Then we would've been looking at a sweep tonight.

Even as it was, after the first inning, Verlander pitched what was probably as good a game as he has pitched for Detroit. He made two bad pitches in that first inning and it cost him on the home run to Jim Thome, but the rest of that game he was just outstanding.

He was a thrower in that first inning and a pitcher the rest of the game. But it didn't matter because we only scored one run all night.

We should have won the first game in this series, and we should have won that second one, with Verlander pitching, too. That would have made our win tonight really something. It certainly would have given the White Sox something to think about.

We played good enough to sweep this series. We really did, and we knew it, but we only got one win to show for it. When you are grinding gears the way we have been, that's what happens. Even with the bad start we had back at the beginning of the season, we could be knocking on the door right now. We could be four games back or three back or even closer, but we're not.

That's been the theme this year. We *could have been* or we *should have been*. We seem to get fully dressed, but we forget our belt or we leave our shoes untied. We just don't ever seem to complete the whole picture.

A sweep would have really pushed us forward, mentally, into the second half of August, which I think is the hardest part of the season. They call them the *dog days* for a reason. That's when you either end up being in the thick of the pennant race or you finally realize you are out of it.

AUGUST 9, 2008
DETROIT, MI

Miguel Cabrera homered twice tonight, driving in four runs, and Gary Sheffield and Edgar Renteria chipped in solo shots as the Tigers overpowered the Oakland A's 10–2 before a delighted Comerica Park sellout of 41,308.

It was the Tigers' 24th sellout of the season and the 21st home game in a row to which the Tigers have attracted 40,000 or more customers—a tribute more to the fans' lofty expectations last winter when those tickets went on sale than to the team's performance this year.

. . . .

Tonight's game was a perfect example of the way we thought this season was going to go. We got hitting, we got pitching, we got everything. That's the team we thought we had, coming out of spring training. We liked our pitching, and we knew we could score a lot of runs.

Miguel Cabrera has really been pounding the ball lately. He's hitting the way he always hit in Florida, the way everybody expected him to hit when we made the trade. I'm sure people were skeptical the first couple months of the year, when he was struggling, but I never doubted that he would hit. You don't hit like Miguel did for the first four years of his big-league career and then suddenly forget how to hit just because you change teams or you change leagues.

The problem is when people look at a big guy like Cabrera, they think he should hit like that all the time, and it just doesn't happen that way.

But I'll make a prediction: at some point in the next five years, as Cabrera gets older and wiser and more accustomed to this league, he is going to have a season offensively like nobody around here has ever seen before. Miguel Cabrera is going to do some things that have never been done before in a Detroit uniform.

As for this season, the numbers speak for themselves. We've lost a lot of games lately when our pitching let us down, and we've lost a lot of games when we didn't get the clutch hits with men on base to score runs the way we should have.

Coming out of spring training, I would have bet my year's salary that we wouldn't be shut out five times all year, and so far we've been shut out 11. It defies logic.

When we have gotten good pitching, too many times we haven't gotten the hits we needed, and when the hitting has been there, we haven't gotten the pitching.

We knew coming into the season that we weren't the type of team that was going to shut a lot of people out. Nobody expected us to do that. We figured our pitchers would hold the other side to four or five runs most nights and we'd score six or seven. But, all too often, one or the other just hasn't happened.

AUGUST 11, 2008
DETROIT, MI

Gary Sheffield was back at the center of another controversy today over comments he made in an interview with the *Boston Globe* in which he again expressed his dislike for being a designated hitter, complained about being a "platoon player" this year, and claimed his current role deprives him of the opportunity to be the "vocal" team leader that he would like to be.

"I can't talk to guys from the bench because I don't feel right about it," the 39-year-old Sheffield said. "I'm in a role now where I don't know what to do, really. I just sit down and hit."

Jim Leyland read Sheffield's comments and immediately fired back. "I was totally flabbergasted by that article," the manager said before tonight's game. "I'm shocked. I'm befuddled by it. I was blindsided by it.

"You lead by example, by playing hard, by playing the game right. Bust your butt, that's how you lead. You don't lead by yelling.

"Gary Sheffield leads by knocking in runs and pounding the ball," Leyland continued. "That's the kind of leader he has always been. That's the kind of leader I want.

"Maybe a little more production would help," Leyland added.

Leyland disputed Sheffield's claim that he has been "platooned" at DH.

"He played 36 of 43 games since he came off the DL [June 24]," Leyland said. "Anybody who has got a f*cking brain knows that's not a platoon. Gary Sheffield has never been platooned since he's been here."

Sheffield, who has one year remaining on his contract, which calls for a salary of $14 million in 2009, has started 19 of the Tigers' 23 games since the All-Star break—all as their DH. He has hit five home runs and driven in 15 runs in those 20 games, compared with five home runs and 18 RBIs in his first 55 games. He is currently batting .222.

Sheffield stood by his comments. "I come here some days and I play, and some days I don't play; that's a platoon to me," the aging slugger said. "If you're an every-day player, you play every day. I don't see why I need to rest to DH."

Sheffield was upset because Leyland had been rotating him, Marcus Thames, and Matt Joyce as designated hitter in an effort to get all three of them playing time—but Thames and Joyce also played left field.

"I'm capable of playing the outfield right now," Sheffield said. "My arm feels great. If I feel good, I have the right to say I feel good."

However, Leyland strongly disputed Sheffield's claim that he can still play the outfield. Sheffield has not played the outfield since May 16, when it was decided his ailing right shoulder made him a defensive liability.

"I tried to play him [Sheffield] in the outfield this year and it didn't work," Leyland said. "He couldn't throw the ball in from the outfield.

"I understand he'd rather play the outfield, but I've had medical people tell me it's suicidal for me to try to play him in the outfield right now," Leyland declared.

Furthermore, Leyland said he was "totally caught off guard" by Sheffield's statement that, "I don't want to DH."

"Before we made the trade for Gary Sheffield [in November 2006], we received permission from the commissioner's office to speak with Gary, and I told him then, 'All I have for you here is the DH role and maybe you can play the outfield once in a while,'" Leyland recalled.

"I told him, 'If you can't accept that, don't come here, don't approve the trade.' He was made aware of the fact that he was going to be the DH here, period. That was decided before the trade was ever made. So what's the point?

"He's been here a year and three-quarters, and all of sudden he doesn't want to DH? Gary Sheffield is the DH here. That's what he is.

"I'm sure he is frustrated," Leyland said. "But I've been a Gary Sheffield sup-porter since day one. I've had as good a relationship with Gary as I've had with any player. I've never had a conversation with Gary Sheffield when he said he's unhappy with his role.

"You're talking about a veteran player who has been brutally banged up. And he's still playing. The lack of production for Gary this year is due to injuries. Injuries have not permitted him to do the things he's done in the past.

"I feel bad that he has had these injuries," Leyland added. "That's not his fault. But it's not Jim Leyland's fault, either."

.   .   .   .

Gary Sheffield is a very prideful guy who has played this game for 20 years. I know nobody feels worse about what has happened to him this year than Gary Sheffield does. He's frustrated, and he's had some physical issues that have made this season even more frustrating.

He's not consistently hitting the ball as hard as he did before he got hurt last year. I don't know if that's part mental or part physical or part mechanical. Maybe it's all three. But if there is a way he can bounce back and still compete the way he used to, Gary Sheffield will figure it out.

I don't know if he's physically finished or not. Only he knows that. Maybe getting some rest during the off-season and working hard, like he always does, can make a difference. I do know this much: I'd like to have him back next year so we can find out just how good he can still be.

I think Gary wants to prove—to himself first of all, and then to the Tigers and to everybody else—that he can still get it done at this level.

AUGUST 14, 2008
DETROIT, MI

Before the Tigers took the field this afternoon, Jim Leyland gathered his team and repeated a message to the group that he has been preaching to players individually for days: "Don't give in."

After the game, Leyland shared the details of his brief pep talk with the media.

"I told 'em, 'I'm going to manage my butt off for this last month and a half, and I want you to play your butts off for the last month and a half,'" Leyland said. "I told 'em, 'Let's see what we've got. Let's have fun.'"

The dreaded "dog days of August" can be especially hard on a team that is losing the way the Tigers have been. That was why Leyland felt the need to speak out.

"We've got a lot of pride here; I wanted to make sure we didn't get lulled to sleep," the manager explained.

After the Tigers rallied for five runs after two were out in the eighth inning to halt their latest winning streak with a 5–1 matinee win over Toronto as rookie Armando Galarraga raised his record to a surprising 11–4, some of the players admitted Leyland's message came through loud and clear.

"There was a reason behind him having that meeting," said Brandon Inge. "Obviously, he saw something. I got his point. You can't play all pent up and worried about everything."

"Let's face it, we're still long shots," Leyland acknowledged. "But we're not out of it. I'm certainly not giving up the ship. I'm not saying we can't win, not by any means, but you can feel the division slipping away. I can't stand up there and tell my players, 'We're going to win this thing.' They'd just look at me.

"The thing you always worry about, as a manager, is what the perception is," Leyland admitted. "People look at your team and say, 'They've given up.'

"Players don't mean it, but psychologically, you just give in sometimes," he said. "It's important for the players to remember you can't always have a great performance—but you can have a great effort.

"You can't give up just because it's August 14ᵗʰ, " Leyland said. "You can't get trapped into thinking, *Well it's just not our year*. That's what we've got to guard against right now: subconsciously giving in. Number one, because you are getting paid to do your job, and number two, because people paid to see you do your job.

"We're going to do our best to give the fans their money's worth," Leyland vowed. "They're spending hard-earned money, and we're making big money. We're going to get crowds of 30,000 or more pretty much every night the rest of the year. We owe 'em something."

Today, for a change, the Tigers gave those fans their money's worth.

· · · ·

Every time Jim has a meeting, it serves a purpose. He doesn't just call a meeting to be having a meeting. When a manager does that, the meetings lose their value.

Today's wasn't a shock-value meeting; it was just a reminder that there is a lot of baseball left. And we've still got a shot. Stranger things have happened. But more than anything else, he told the players, "It's a privilege to be up here in the big leagues."

He told them, "Just try to enjoy yourselves as much as possible these last six weeks."

Jim knows that if you let a season get away from you, it can get awfully ugly awfully quickly.

This team has sold a lot of tickets for the home games that we have left. And those fans expect to see their team walk away with a win when they come to the ballpark, regardless of where we happen to be in the standings. They want to come to the ballpark and watch the hometown team win. Everybody does. That's true with every team in every town in baseball. We owe the fans that much. We can't just show up, punch a time card, and put in our time. We owe it to them to try as hard as we can to win every night. That was what Jim was reminding us about.

We need to create a happy atmosphere and a winning atmosphere, regardless of where we are in the standings. That's very important, especially at this point in the season and with the situation we're in.

We've still got to come to the ballpark and take the field every day with the attitude that we're still in the pennant race—even if, realistically, it looks like we're not.

AUGUST 18, 2008
ARLINGTON, TX

Belated rallies in the seventh and eighth innings and solid pitching against his former team by Kenny Rogers, who snapped a personal four-game losing streak plus a save from new closer Fernando Rodney, proved to be just enough as the Tigers edged the Texas Rangers tonight, 8–7.

Gary Sheffield belted a historic two-run homer, the 493rd of his career, tying him with the legendary Lou Gehrig and Fred McGriff, and Curtis Granderson knocked in four runs with a pair of triples, giving him nine three-baggers for the year and a shot at leading the league in that always-exciting department for the second year in a row.

The last Tiger to lead the American League in triples in back-to-back seasons was the legendary speedster Ty Cobb in 1917–18.

· · · ·

The funny thing about this club is they have never rolled over and given up after losing a game like we did against Baltimore (16–8) on Sunday. They keep bouncing back. I've said for two months that we've had a lot of reasons to give up, but we haven't done that.

We've had a lot of bad losses this year, a lot of mentally draining losses, but these guys show up at the ballpark every day ready to play and determined to win. And let me tell you, as a former player, that's a hard thing to do.

The biggest thing that the average fan and the guys in the media don't understand is how hard this game is to play, how hard the season is, even for a guy who has a three- or four-year contract. You might think it would be easy, but it's not. Your body is hurting, maybe you're in a slump, your team's not playing well—those things all add up, especially late in the season.

The hardest thing about playing this game at this level is not the physical side, it's the mental aspect of it. Your body is going to follow whatever your mind tells it. If your mind tells your body to do something, your body will respond. That's why you hear all those crazy stories about women being able to lift up cars when their husbands are trapped and dying under them after accidents.

These guys and any guy who has ever played the game, including myself, understand that the challenge is not hitting a fastball—the challenge is getting ready to hit that fastball. The physical part of hitting the ball is secondary to the mental part of preparing to hit it. For any athlete, not just baseball players, the critical part is preparing for the competition.

Pride in yourself is a big motivator. Fear of failure is another. Guys are motivated for different reasons. Personally, I hated to lose. I hated to let anybody beat me. I always wanted to beat the guy I was up against. When I got to first base, I wanted to beat the pitcher and the catcher and steal second. When I was playing the outfield and there was a guy on second base, I wanted to prove to him that he was stupid if he tried to score on me.

You're always playing those types of mind games. That's the challenge in this game.

And the best part of this season has been the fact that this ballclub has been up to that part of the challenge. I know it hasn't always looked that way. When you lose to Baltimore on a Sunday afternoon in August and you've just given up four million runs, it doesn't look like you're up to the challenge. But that's not the case. We just haven't executed on a consistent basis this year—defensively, offensively, or pitching-wise. We just haven't.

Speaking of Kenny Rogers, it doesn't happen so much down here in Texas because Kenny played here and the fans here know him, but everywhere else we go on the road, I always get a lot of, "Hey, Kenny Rogers!" It's always,

"Kenny, can I have your autograph? Will you sign this, Kenny?" I even hear it in spring training. People mistake me for him all the time. It's ridiculous. Maybe it's because both of us have that 5 o'clock shadow going. And we're both good looking, obviously. Sometimes I say, "I'll sign when I start throwing left-handed," and sometimes I'll sign my name *Kenny Rogers* just to shut them up. But I do it left-handed, so it's not very legible.

I let them figure it out when they get home.

AUGUST 19, 2008
ARLINGTON, TX

Armando Galarraga, who joined the Tigers organization in February in a then–seemingly insignificant minor-league trade with the Texas Rangers for outfielder Michael Hernandez, who is no longer even in baseball, got a chance tonight to show the Rangers what a mistake they made last winter.

And Galarraga made the most of the opportunity, riding a pair of home runs from fellow rookie Matt Joyce to his 12th win of the season, 11–3.

•   •   •   •

Armando Galarraga has certainly been the guy who has potentially saved our hide this year. If he had come up in April and hadn't done the job, who knows what might have happened. We might be a whole lot worse off than we are right now. And the Texas Rangers might find themselves in the wild-card race right now, if they still had him. You never know how things are going to turn out; that's the beauty of baseball.

It's scary how well Armando has pitched for us this year. The really scary thing is how everybody could miss on him, how everybody could be so wrong about one guy in such a very short period of time.

As a manager or a general manager or as a coach or a player, if you're not constantly humbled in this game, I think you must really be a stupid person. Because you just can't be right all the time. You can't be good all the time.

The Texas Rangers, a team that desperately needs pitching, completely missed on Armando. They let him go in February for a minor-league outfielder named Michael Hernandez who I believe is now out of baseball.

And in March, Galarraga was one of the first guys we sent back to the minors in the first round of cuts during spring training. And he ended up being our best starting pitcher this year. That is incredible. We brought Armando up in April to take Dontrelle Willis' place, and now he's 12–4. If Dontrelle Willis was 12–4, everybody would be saying, "He's having a heckuva year."

Galarraga throws strike one. That's the key for him. When you're a hitter and you're facing a pitcher who is having a hard time finding the strike zone, you know he is just as apt to throw a pitch a foot outside as he is to throw a strike right down the middle. So as a hitter, you don't have to gear yourself up to look for a pitch on the inside corner or the outside corner. You just gear yourself to look for a pitch that's right down the middle of the plate, something you can jump on and drive.

But when a guy like Galarraga gets strike one on you, now you have to pick a corner. Where is he going to put the next pitch? You have to either pick "in" or "out." You have to try to guess where he's going to throw it; that makes it a lot harder on you as a hitter. You know he's not going to throw you a pitch right down the middle of the plate, and you know he's not going to throw a pitch that's three feet outside. It's going to be down, and it's either going to be on the inside corner or on the outside corner. You have to try to guess which way he's going to go. That's what makes him so effective: he's not afraid to throw strikes.

After the way we played against Baltimore at home last Sunday, when we got clobbered 16–8, I was really fearful of playing these next three games down here in Texas. I was afraid of what might happen to our pitching staff because Texas is a really good hitting team and this is a good hitting ballpark. These guys can really swing the bat and score runs, and this is a ballpark that plays small, even though the dimensions are large. So I was worried about what might happen. But we came from behind to win the first game, and Galarraga pitched a gem tonight.

Matt Joyce is another guy who had no chance to make our team in spring training. Now he's got 12 home runs for us. He's become a very dangerous hitter at times. His biggest issue, as it is with any young player, is consistency. He has shown signs of brilliance, and he has also shown signs of being a rookie.

Is he going to be a great player? No one, including myself, is smart enough to figure that one out. I think only Matt Joyce can answer that question. But he has certainly gotten off to a good start. He's headed in the right direction. He's done some things that make you take notice.

AUGUST 22, 2008
KANSAS CITY, MO

Following a closed-door meeting with Nate Robertson and pitching coach Chuck Hernandez this afternoon, Jim Leyland announced that the struggling left-hander, who served up five home runs in less than four innings in Wednesday night's lopsided 9–1 loss to the Texas Rangers, has been removed from the starting rotation and will pitch in relief while he tries to rediscover his slider and straighten himself out.

Robertson, who signed a three-year, $21.25 million contract extension last winter, is 7–10 and has won just one of his last 11 starts.

"In my mind, I'm still a legit starting pitcher in the big leagues," said Robertson as he stood in the dugout before tonight's game, clearly shaken by the demotion. "This is probably the lowest point for me that I've ever had to deal with. But I think I've bottomed out."

"Skip [Leyland] has got a job to do. He's got to do what's best for this club. After what happened in Texas, he can't feel good about me going out there. I don't feel good about me going out there. I'm just another part of the story this year. It's been frustrating for a lot of people."

"I think it is obvious Nate is not going out there with all of his weapons right now," Leyland explained. "Without his slider, I just can't keep sending him out there all the time. His slider was a big weapon for him, and right now he doesn't have it."

At the conclusion of the 2006 World Series, Jim Leyland called Nate Robertson "the most improved pitcher" on the Tigers' staff. But in 2008 Robertson slumped to 7–11 with a 6.35 ERA—the highest by any regular starting pitcher in the American League—and was removed from the rotation.

．　．　．　．

I don't know if Nate Robertson looks at it this way or if the fans or the media look at it this way, but I think we're really doing the guy a favor by taking him out of the rotation right now. To keep sending him out there to get his brains beat in would be doing a disservice to him.

He's got to figure out how to get hitters out again on a consistent basis. Going to the bullpen, he can come in for one or two innings at a time, get people out, and get himself straightened out. Plus this break might take a little stress off his arm and get him freshened up for next season.

We'd like to get back to the old Nate Robertson that everybody expected to see this year. The Nate Robertson we have been seeing lately is not the Nate Robertson the Tigers want to see—or the Nate Robertson that he wants to be.

AUGUST 24, 2008
KANSAS CITY, MO

With a sweep within their grasp after winning the first two games of this series against the Royals, thanks in part to three gigantic home runs by Miguel Cabrera, the Tigers reverted to form this afternoon, blowing an early three-run lead and losing 7–3.

"This is the kind of game you've got to nail down," Jim Leyland admitted. "We already had two wins. Then we got a three-run lead today. We came out smoking. We had a lot of things going for us.

"But all of a sudden, we got the yips for some reason. We made too many mistakes. You can't give a team extra outs at the major-league level, in Little

League, or wherever. We let this game get away, and you can't do that when you're trying to catch up.

"Obviously, at this point, we're a huge long shot," Leyland acknowledged when asked about the Tigers' fast-fading pennant hopes.

"I'm not going to sit here and say we're going to win 18 in a row and the White Sox and Twins are both going to lose eight in a row. You're whistling 'Dixie' if you think we're going to leap over two teams like that. It's very unlikely both of them are going to go into some fantastic funk. I'm not going to stand up in front of my team and say, 'We're going to win this thing.' They'd look at me like I was crazy. I'd lose all credibility if I said that.

"But are we going to try to do that?" Leyland added. "Absolutely."

· · · ·

When you're having a season like the one we're having, one particular game or one series can be a microcosm of the year you're having. That was certainly the case today. We had the kind of offensive lapse and defensive lapse and pitching lapse that we've been having all year.

When the season is not going the way you want it go, the way you expected it to go, the season exposes your weaknesses. That's why you play for six months. You find out who the good teams are, the teams that don't have those weaknesses, and you identify those teams that end up playing out the season the way we are.

The hardest part of this time of the year, when you're in the position that we're in, is knowing that you're just playing out the season. I felt that as a player, and I can feel it now. That's where you need your professionalism to take over.

This is when you need to show up at the ballpark every day with the right attitude. You don't want to just punch a clock and put in your time. You don't want to show up not caring whether you win or lose that night. It's still important to come to the ballpark every day and prepare to win, because that's what we're paid to do.

All those clichés that have been uttered for decades become reality for a player or a ballclub that is out of contention at this time of the year.

We started this season, on paper, as a good team. Expectations were high. But we actually started off this season as a bad team. When you start the year 0–7 and then 2–10 the way we did, that's not the sign of a good team. Good teams don't go 0–7 or 2–10. All those weaknesses that showed up at the beginning of the season reared their ugly heads throughout the season, too, and they're still showing up. And they will continue to show up because those issues have to be resolved or we'll have another year like this one.

Now we're going home to play Cleveland. And instead of battling the Indians for first place the way everybody thought we would be doing when they looked at the schedule back in spring training, we're fighting over third place.

But there are no bronze medals in baseball.

AUGUST 27, 2008
DETROIT, MI

Fighting back the tears, struggling to maintain his composure, Todd Jones forced himself to smile as he addressed his teammates this afternoon then walked around the clubhouse hugging them one by one, shaking their hands, and saying good-bye. After 16 seasons and 319 saves—a team-record 235 of them in two tours of duty with the Tigers—the 40-year-old reliever has probably pitched his last game, at least in Detroit.

"I'm going home, try to rehab and get better, and see if I can come back," Jones said as he cleaned out his corner locker, packing all of his personal belongings in a large equipment bag.

Jones, who was 4–1 this season with a team-high 18 saves and a 4.97 ERA, has been on the disabled list since August 16 with a sore shoulder.

Although the emotional Jones has repeatedly dodged the subject of retirement, it appears unlikely he will pitch again this season, if ever.

Jones' $7 million, one-year contract with the Tigers expires at the end of the season. And although he will be a free agent, it is difficult to imagine him signing with another team for next year.

"Whether he'll pitch again or not is the big question mark," Jim Leyland admitted. "I don't foresee him being ready to pitch again this year at this point."

On Monday, Jones, who did not accompany the team on its recent road trip to Texas and Kansas City, underwent an arthrogram, during which dye was injected into his injured right shoulder. "My rotator cuff is a little bit frayed, and I've still got a torn labrum from 2006," Jones explained.

Obviously, this was not the way Jones, 14th all-time in saves, wanted his career to end.

·   ·   ·   ·

It is unfortunate that Todd Jones has to close out the career he has had in a season like this. It's been a tough season, and it's a tough way to end a career.

You hate to see a guy who has been as successful as Todd end his career with an injury after pitching poorly.

Today was hard for Todd. Very hard. He is a very emotional guy, but that was part of what made Todd the success that he was. He cared so much. He cared so much about being a professional and about being a good teammate. Todd Jones was a unique closer in the sense that he had a lot of warmth and caring in his soul. A lot of closers are seen as being coldhearted. That's what makes them good.

But Todd was just the opposite. He suffered every time he lost a game. He was part of the high expectations this year for this team being in the pennant race. He expected it, and we expected it. We expected him to be the Todd Jones who has been so effective, not only here but other places, in past years.

For Todd personally, this season has sort of been like our season as a team: short-lived and with a sad ending.

AUGUST 29, 2008
DETROIT, MI

Kenny Rogers called it "a joke" and predicted it will "open up a whole Pandora's box." Brandon Inge predicted it will "crush" baseball and said, "Babe Ruth and Ted Williams must be rolling over in their graves."

They were talking about instant replay, which made its debut at Comerica Park tonight as the Tigers downed the Kansas City Royals, 6–3.

For the time being, anyway, instant replay will be limited to reviewing questionable home runs: Did a fly ball actually go over the fence? Was the ball fair or foul? Was there fan interference?

"Where does it stop?" Inge wondered. "Before long it will be balls and strikes. Then close plays at home plate. Then close plays at first base and second and third."

"Even though I might disagree with some of the calls that are made, that's part of the game," Rogers said. "That's the beauty of the game—its imperfection. Now they want to take that away. I think the game is pretty good the way it is, the way it has been for the last 100 years.

"How far does it have to go to be fair? If they're going to make it fair for the hitters, shouldn't they make it fair for the pitchers, too?"

· · · ·

I'm not in favor of instant replay at all. Just because you can do something, just because you have the technology that lets you do something, doesn't mean you should do it.

I love the tradition of the game. Like it or not, the umpires are a big part of this game. They always have been. Not that they want to be noticed or that they even should be noticed, but the umpires in baseball have a bigger impact on the sport than a referee does in basketball or a linesman does in football. This is especially true of the umpire working behind home plate. He's the balls-and-strikes guy; he's in control of the game.

If you are going to delegate that much control of the game to four people for so long and then suddenly yank some of that control away just because they might get one or two calls wrong the entire year doesn't make sense to me. I just don't see the sanity in it.

The umpires are right 99.9 percent of the time. If you look at 1,000 calls that the umpires make over the course of a season, they're right 999 times.

My gosh. Part of the beauty of this game, to me, is its imperfection. Players make mistakes. Managers make mistakes. Coaches make mistakes. And once in a while, an umpire makes a mistake. We're all human, and the fans love to second-guess us.

Believe me, it's a very slippery slope. I'm telling you, within five years, we'll see instant replay moving into the infield to cover close plays there, too. Look at the NFL. Pro football totally relies on instant replay now. I hate it. I think it's terrible. It disrupts the whole flow of the game.

I don't know if I will still be in the game when instant replay moves into the infield in baseball, as it surely will, but I know one thing: I won't be watching it.

Chapter 8

SEPTEMBER

"A Bad, Ugly, Underachieving Team"

SEPTEMBER 1, 2008
DETROIT, MI

Even Miguel Cabrera's 30th home run of the season—making him just the sixth player in Tigers history, the first since Bobby Higginson in 2000, and the youngest since 24-year-old Hank Greenberg in 1935, to smack 30 or more homers, knock in 100 or more runs and deliver at least 30 doubles in the same season—wasn't enough to enable the Tigers to overcome their hideous start on this holiday afternoon.

The Tigers, who trailed the New York Yankees, 11–2, before they got a chance to bat for the third time, battled back and eventually made the game interesting as they have so often done this season, before falling, 13–9, in a makeup game that marked the return to Detroit of popular departed catcher Pudge Rodriguez.

The names of Hank Greenberg, Rocky Colavito, Rudy York, Tony Clark, and Bobby Higginson mean nothing to Cabrera. But if Miguel's first season in Detroit is any indication, his name will mean plenty to Tigers fans for many years to come.

Greenberg put together seasons of 30 home runs, 100 RBIs, and 30 doubles four times during his Hall of Fame career. Colavito did it in back-to-back years in 1961–1962. In 108 years of Tigers baseball, only York (1940), Clark (1998), Higginson, and now Cabrera have also stacked up numbers like that.

How good can Miguel Cabrera be?

"I don't know," Cabrera admitted after today's game, smiling. "You tell me."

"He's been one of the biggest forces in baseball for his first five years in the history of the game," manager Jim Leyland raved. "If we can get him to go up to the plate with that same concentration on a more consistent basis, there's no telling what this guy can do. He's one of the premier offensive players in the game."

Nothing brings out the best in Cabrera like the sight of teammates on the base paths and the realization that a ballgame is on the line. "He's at his best when it really means something," Leyland said.

"I think different when I see that," admitted Cabrera, who is batting .467 with 17 RBIs in bases-loaded situations this season. "I say to myself, 'I have to.'

"If you don't do it, you feel bad. I like to feel good."

Cabrera's numbers speak for themselves: 30 home runs, 106 RBIs, 31 doubles—with a month of the season yet to play. And he is only 25 years old, a baby in baseball terms.

"He could put up A-Rod numbers," slugger Gary Sheffield predicted, referring to the Yankees' future Hall of Famer Alex Rodriguez. "The sky's the limit."

Cabrera has now topped 100 RBIs for five seasons in a row. Only two Tigers, Harry Heilmann in 1923–1929 and Charlie Gehringer in 1932–1936 ever did that. And they're both in the Hall of Fame. Of course, Cabrera's first four 100-RBI seasons came as a member of the Florida Marlins.

·   ·   ·   ·

I don't know what happened to Miguel Cabrera during the first half of the year. He got off to a slow start. He just didn't hit well. But I knew one thing all along: he wasn't going to stay in that slump forever. His track record in Florida speaks for itself. I wasn't worried about him not hitting.

A lot of things entered into the equation for Miguel this year. He signed that big contract last spring and, human nature being what it is, some people handle situations like that differently than other people do. People who read about sports or watch sports or listen to sports often don't understand the human element that is involved.

Everybody handles their contract situations in a different manner. Some guys press when they get a big contract and they don't play as well. Some guys, when they are in their free-agent year, going for a big contract, play better than they did in previous years. Some guys play worse in that situation because they're trying too hard. That is something you can never anticipate when it comes to professional athletes.

As I said before, I don't think we've seen the real Miguel Cabrera yet. He is one of the few guys we have who is capable of carrying this team offensively. If we got good pitching, Miguel Cabrera could carry this club for two weeks. No question about it. He can drive in a run and we win 2–1, or he can drive in four runs and we win 4–3. That is the capacity he has: big hits and big home runs.

One of these years, Cabrera is going to put together a full season like he has had during the second half of this year. And when he does that, he is going to have some unbelievable numbers. He is going to put up numbers that have never been seen before in a Detroit Tigers uniform.

SEPTEMBER 2, 2008
DETROIT, MI

The Tigers' glaring lack of speed, long a lamentable tradition in Detroit in spite of the legacy of Ty Cobb, reared its ugly head again tonight as the Los Angeles Angels were able to manufacture a run in the final inning while the Tigers were not. The result was a 5–4 loss.

Jim Leyland knew his team was in trouble when, with the score tied at 4–4 thanks to Miguel Cabrera's three hits and three RBIs, closer Fernando Rodney walked Angels speedster Chone Figgins to begin the top half of the ninth inning.

"The walk was the thing that killed us," Leyland admitted later. "You know, if Figgins gets on base, that's a potential run. A walk there was the kiss of death, because Figgins has speed."

As expected, Figgins stole second, advanced to third on Garret Anderson's ground out, and crossed the plate with what turned out to be the winning run on Mark Teixeira's sacrifice fly.

The Tigers also got their leadoff hitter, Edgar Renteria, aboard in the bottom half of the ninth. Renteria also swiped second—although not with nearly as much certainty as Figgins had.

But Renteria advanced no further as Curtis Granderson walked and Placido Polanco grounded out to end the game.

"We try to run," Leyland said, shaking his head. "But when we run, we hold our nuts."

. . . .

Stealing bases is something we are not going to lead the league in. We're just not. There's no question about that. But we knew that coming in. We knew way back in March that this team wasn't going to score runs based on speed. We knew we needed to hit the ball—and hit it a lot harder than we have, especially early in the year, in order to score runs. Our lack of speed is an anchor that we have carried around all year.

There are two kinds of speed. There is what I call "track speed" and there is "baseball speed." We really only have one guy who has baseball speed, and that's Curtis Granderson. We don't have anybody with track speed. I'm sure that's a subject that will be addressed in the off-season. If it can be fixed, it will be.

None of our players is going to get faster from this year to next. That's not going to happen. But it could be a matter of changing a player or two at a particular position and hopefully gaining some speed in the process.

I do think we have a couple of weapons that we need to take better advantage of in certain situations. One is where the opposing pitcher is slow to the plate with his delivery. I'm talking about 1.4 seconds or longer. With a good lead and a good jump, if the pitcher is taking 1.4 seconds to throw the ball, it doesn't matter who is behind the plate or how good the catcher's arm is. You should be able to steal that base.

It all starts with your head. A lot of people don't realize this, but the fastest moving part of your body is your head. You think it's your feet, but it's not. Your head can move faster than any other part. You've got to remember, your body is going to follow wherever your head goes. In everything you do in life, your head moves first, then your torso moves, then your legs move. If you can move your head quickly, the rest of your body will come along.

It sounds kind of silly, but I tell players, "If you practice moving your head as you practice getting your jumps off first base, your body will react." You have to do it often enough in practice so that when the game starts, it becomes a natural move, just like breathing.

I try to get base-stealers to move their heads quickly, to flick their heads or rotate their heads toward second base or back to first base. You rotate your head as fast as you can to second base if you're going, and you rotate your head back to your left if you have to get back to first base. You focus on the outside corner of the base. If you focus on the big part of the bag, you're going to end up putting your hand in the middle of the bag, which is an easier tag for the fielder. I want the runner to focus on the outside part of the bag, which is the furthest point from home plate.

If that's where your right hand ends up, on the very corner of the outside part of the base, the tag ends up being another six inches to a foot longer for the fielder. That can make the difference between being safe or out.

But it all starts with your head.

SEPTEMBER 12, 2008
CHICAGO, IL

The star-crossed career of Joel Zumaya, the Tigers' rock-star reliever with the blazing fastball, has hit yet another bump in the road.

Zumaya, who has been on the disabled list since August 13, will be shut down from all further baseball activity for the next six to eight weeks because of a hairline fracture that was discovered yesterday in the coracoid bone in the front of his right shoulder.

According to Tigers head athletic trainer Kevin Rand, Zumaya, who appeared in just 21 games this season after undergoing reconstructive shoulder surgery last fall, felt pain in his shoulder when he woke up yesterday. The Tigers sent him to see team physician Dr. Stephen Lemos. X-rays and an MRI revealed a nondisplaced stress fracture in his shoulder.

Rand said he believes the crack in the bone was a recent occurrence during Zumaya's ongoing rehab. "He threw light sessions on the sidelines on Monday and Tuesday and he felt fine," the trainer said prior to tonight's rainout against the White Sox.

"It's hard to say when this happened," Rand explained. "Joel's shoulder surgery was extremely unique, and this rehab has been a totally unique situation. This latest injury is a product of him coming back."

Jim Leyland had hoped that Zumaya, who left the game on August 9 after adhesions in his surgically repaired shoulder broke loose, might be able to pitch in a game or two before the season ends in order to give the high-strung hurler some peace of mind this winter. Leyland also hoped to have Zumaya pitch in the Instructional League this fall to build up his arm strength.

Both of those options are now out of the question, placing Zumaya's status next spring, at least at the start of training camp, in doubt.

Zumaya, who has been injured during each of his three seasons in the big leagues, was 0–2 with a 3.47 ERA this year. But he never got into a groove, walking 22 batters in 23⅓ innings.

In 2006 Zumaya was sidelined with a freak finger injury suffered while playing a video game. Last season he underwent surgery after rupturing a tendon in the middle finger on his right hand and appeared in just 28 games. Last fall, while removing boxes from his parents' attic in anticipation of advancing wildfires near their San Diego home, he severely separated his shoulder, necessitating major surgery.

.   .   .   .

When I was playing in the National League with the Cardinals and Pirates, Wrigley Field here in Chicago was by far my favorite ballpark. Part of it was the proximity to the fans. When I played the outfield at Wrigley, I felt like the fans were right on top of me. And when I was in the on-deck circle, the fans were so close I felt like I could almost turn around and take a bite out of their hot dogs if I had wanted to. You can reach right into their popcorn, provided they're offering.

And as a hitter, at least during the summer months, I always thought Wrigley Field was the best place to hit.

Whenever I traveled to Chicago as a player, and now as a coach with the Tigers, we have always stayed at the Westin Hotel on Michigan Avenue. No place else. And as a player I always tried to get a room facing Lake Michigan. There was a building beyond the hotel that had a flag on top of the roof. I would get up in the morning, open my drapes, and look at that flag to see which way the wind was blowing.

If I opened my curtains and saw that the wind was blowing out toward the lake, I knew I was going to have a good day at Wrigley. I just knew it.

I'd say Chicago is my favorite city in the American League. It's so vibrant. It doesn't matter if we play a day game or a night game, you can always find something to do or someplace to eat after the game. The restaurants here are tremendous.

I like Fenway Park and Boston, too. That's a great venue.

I also like New York, I really do, but the best thing about New York is leaving. Three or four days there is about all I can take.

When I was playing in the National League, I always looked forward to going to San Francisco. Next to Chicago, it was my favorite.

My least favorite ballparks used to be the Astrodome and the old stadium in Montreal. It always felt like you were playing inside King Kong's toilet bowl. The ballpark had a ring around the top, and you felt like you were inside a john.

SEPTEMBER 13, 2008
CHICAGO, IL

The Tigers and White Sox were rained out again today at soggy U.S. Cellular Field. The weather was so bad that many of the players didn't even bother to put their uniforms on.

Jim Leyland, who is a huge Notre Dame fan, immediately went back to his hotel to watch some college football. Brandon Inge chartered an airplane and, despite the storms spawned by the remnants of Hurricane Ike, flew to Virginia to attend his grandfather's funeral. Curtis Granderson paid another visit to the Chicago-area restaurant where he is now a silent partner.

The forecast in Chicago calls for more rain tomorrow, putting this entire three-game weekend series, which means so much to the playoff-minded White Sox, in jeopardy.

When asked today how long he thought the rain would last, Leyland had a simple answer: "Go ask Andy Van Slyke. He's a scratch golfer, he's a meteorologist, and I'm sure he's a good mechanic," the Tigers manager explained. "The only thing he doesn't do well is coach first base."

Then Leyland laughed.

. . . .

I have always been fascinated by the weather. Even as a kid, I would run outside during thunderstorms in upstate New York to watch the lightning and to watch it rain. I loved to ride my bike in the rain. When I was 10, I almost got hit by lightning while I was riding my bike. The lightning shocked my bike. But I was young and dumb and rambunctious. I'm not rambunctious anymore, I'm just stupid.

I'm still fascinated by weather. The thing that amazes me is how little anyone really knows about the weather—about what's happening or what is coming or where it's going.

I'm always reading about the weather or checking out the maps and charts on the Internet. I do my homework. I even did the weather on TV a few times when I was playing in Pittsburgh.

I'm extremely interested in global warming now that it has become a political issue. I know what heats the planet and what cools it. I'm up-to-date on all that.

SEPTEMBER 14, 2008
CHICAGO, IL

Only a two-run, ninth-inning home run by Magglio Ordonez, his 20th homer of the season, saved the Tigers from being shut out in the opener on this dreary Sunday afternoon. After enduring yet another lengthy rain delay, they dropped both ends of their doubleheader against the White Sox, 4–2 and 11–7.

This marks the eighth year in Ordonez's career—and the third in a row as a Tiger—that he has homered 20 or more times.

Ordonez is now hitting .323 in his quest to become the first Tiger to win back-to-back batting titles since Ty Cobb in 1917–1919.

.   .   .   .

That is about as quiet a .323 average as you can have. But Magglio wants that batting title. Trust me, he really wants it. He radiates a laissez faire body language, but, deep down, Magglio really wants to hit. I can see it when he makes an out. He gets a look on his face that says, *The pitcher got away with something there*. He has a lot of pride.

Magglio Ordonez is as good a right-handed hitter as I've ever seen. When he and Miguel Cabrera get it going together, we've got as good a one-two punch as any team in the league.

Magglio Ordonez couldn't repeat his spectacular performance of 2007, but he did bat .317 in 2008—fifth-best in the American League. Ordonez also drove in 103 runs, marking the third year in a row that he topped 100 RBIs—the first Tiger to do that since Cecil Fielder in 1990–1993.

When Magglio swings badly, he hits .300. That would be a bad year for him, hitting .300. When he swings well, he hits .325. And when he has a real good year, he hits .350. That's what you get with him: he's a pure hitter.

If Magglio "struggles" next season as a .320 hitter, I'd be happy to see that.

SEPTEMBER 17, 2008
ARLINGTON, TX

After dropping their first two games in Texas to run their latest losing streak to six in a row, the Tigers clobbered the Rangers tonight, 17–4,

Freddy Garcia, making his first big-league appearance since June 2007, impressed everyone with his performance a year after undergoing major shoulder surgery. "It was like riding a bike for that guy," Jim Leyland marveled.

. . . .

Playing out the rest of the year and winning a lot of games is very important to us for next year. I really believe we can set the tone for next year by the way we finish this year. That doesn't mean that if we lose our last 11 in a row that we're going to be terrible next year. I'm not saying that. But I've played on teams that have had disappointing years but actually finished their seasons pretty well. And then they have gone on to have great seasons the next year.

I can give you a perfect example of that: the Pittsburgh Pirates in 1989 and 1990. In 1989 we had a lot of injuries, and we ended up way under .500 at 74–88 and in fifth place,

19 games behind. But toward the end of the season, we got it together. And I think that had a lot to do with our winning the division the next season when we went 95–67.

Going into a new season, you've got to believe that you have enough talent to compete. And you've got to believe that your team is willing to do what it takes mentally to win ballgames.

Physically and mentally, we have been there this year, especially during the second half of the season. But we've had some injuries and we've had some guys not play up to their full potential. Even though some of these guys won't be back next year—some of them know that already, and some don't know it yet—it is important to send a message now to the fans, to the coaches, to the manager, to the general manager, and to the owner, that this club is going to do whatever it takes to put itself on top next year.

As disappointing as this season has been, that pays dividends. It's very important to these players.

I don't believe the fact that we're probably going to finish under .500 makes a big difference. I've never put much stock in won-lost records. Whether we finish the year in third place or fourth place isn't a big deal for me, either. You can finish second and not have the ingredients on your ballclub to be a winner. But I've been impressed with the way we've played lately; I really have.

Sure, there have been times when it may have looked like we just mailed it in, but I can tell you, there hasn't been one game where we mailed it in. When you get shut out, it looks bad. When you give up 15 runs, it looks bad. But as discouraging as a lot of games have been this year, we've gotten back into a lot of ballgames and kept ourselves in a lot of ballgames after we had fallen behind by a lot of runs.

Sure, we've come up short a lot of times, but we've fought back. We've given up a lot of runs, but we've battled back. We've blown a lot of leads late in ballgames that we've ended up losing, but these guys are still competing. They're not getting used to losing. That's not the case at all. They're still disappointed when we lose.

The competitive nature is there. You can see it. You can feel it. And that's very, very important.

SEPTEMBER 19, 2008
CLEVELAND, OH

Jim Leyland began serving a three-game suspension tonight for what Major League Baseball called "inappropriate conduct" in his arguments with umpires Eric Cooper and Angel Hernandez during and after the Tigers' losses in Texas on Monday and Tuesday.

Gary Sheffield will undoubtedly soon be suspended, too. Sheffield was ejected in the seventh inning of tonight's 6–5 last-inning loss to Cleveland after he was hit on the arm by a pitch from the Indians' Fausto Carmona and charged the mound, setting off a bench-clearing brawl.

After the game, an unrepentant Sheffield, still seething, vowed to seek revenge against Carmona and the other Indians who pummeled him during the melee.

"I watched the tape. I know who the guys are who were punching at the back of my head," Sheffield declared defiantly, the chip clearly visible on his shoulder, as he held court in front of his cubicle in the Tigers clubhouse. "They're going to have to deal with me.

"I wasn't the one hitting the home runs—just because he [Carmona] was upset about somebody [Miguel Cabrera] hitting home runs, why take it out on me?" Sheffield said.

"Any time you do that, you're going to have problems with me. I don't care how big you are.

"It's been happening over and over," Sheffield continued. "This is the third time he [Carmona] has hit me this year.

"Three strikes and out. If there's a fourth strike, it's going to get more violent, trust me."

The records indicate Carmona has actually hit Sheffield with pitches twice this year.

In the top half of the seventh inning, after Miguel Cabrera's second two-run homer of the night off Carmona had put the Tigers on top, 4–2, Carmona plunked Sheffield.

Glaring at Carmona, Sheffield walked slowly to first base, bat still in hand. "I was telling myself, 'Stay cool, don't do nothing,'" Sheffield said later.

"But there is another side of me that wanted to do something," he admitted.

When Carmona threw over to first base in a token pickoff attempt, Sheffield gestured at him to throw the ball toward home plate. Sheffield shouted at the pitcher, the pitcher shouted back, then Sheffield charged the mound, where Carmona moved to meet him.

"He [Carmona] called me out, and I answered the call," Sheffield said. "He gestured at me to come get him. And I was coming."

As the players from both benches and bullpens rushed on to the field, Sheffield grabbed Carmona in a bear hug, admittedly trying to hurl him to the ground, while Carmona's teammates pounded on the back of Sheffield's head. Sheffield later identified Asdrubal Cabrera as one of the Indians who punched him.

Eventually, Tigers coaches Gene Lamont, Chuck Hernandez, and Gene Roof pushed and pulled the enraged Sheffield off the field and into the dugout while the umpires restored order.

Sheffield, Carmona, Placido Polanco, and Cleveland catcher Victor Martinez, who had to be restrained first by Polanco, then by Magglio Ordonez and Miguel Cabrera, were all ejected.

. . . .

My view of tonight's fight was the same as my view of most baseball brawls has always been. I think Gary Sheffield and Fausto Carmona should have just gone at it by themselves. I never jumped on anybody or sucker-punched anybody in my life, and I never would. What took place on the field tonight should have been between Fausto Carmona and Gary Sheffield.

Let the two of them take care of business. Of course, that's never the way it happens. The benches empty and the bullpens empty, and it sometimes ends up being a lot uglier than it would have been if everybody had just let the two guys involved go at it.

I think all of the players should form a big circle and keep pushing the two combatants back to the middle. That's the way I'd like to see these things happen.

I knew Gary was going for Carmona as soon as he got to first base, and I wasn't about to try to stop him. That's Gary's business. I said, "Stay back! Stay back!" but I don't think he even heard me.

Gary was in a total rage by the time he got to first base, and in some ways I don't blame him. When Carmona hit him, it certainly looked to me like it was intentional. When Carmona threw over to first base, he was just rubbing it in.

I heard Gary holler a few choice words at Carmona, and I knew things were going to get ugly. And I wasn't going to get in Gary's way.

These guys are too young and too strong, and I'm too old to be doing that.

SEPTEMBER 21, 2008
CLEVELAND, OH

Dontrelle Willis, one of the pitchers the Tigers are still hoping can fill one of the three pending vacancies in their starting rotation next season, pitched a woeful 2⅓ innings this afternoon, walking six Indians, allowing six runs, and throwing three wild pitches as Cleveland completed its three-game sweep, 10–5.

Willis, acquired last December in the ballyhooed Miguel Cabrera deal and given a new three-year, $29 million contract by the Tigers, is now 0–2. In 19 innings, he has walked 32 batters.

"At times, we were pleasantly surprised; I wouldn't say it was a step back for him," insisted hitting coach Lloyd McClendon, who is filling in as manager while Jim Leyland serves his suspension. "There was some progress there. We just need to get him out there on a consistent basis."

The Tigers had better hope Willis can return to some semblance of his former 22-game-winner self next season. Because, as Leyland admitted before today's game, the Tigers cannot count on another blockbuster trade or another bundle of owner Mike Ilitch's cash to bail the team out of this mess.

"You just can't keep going to the bank," Leyland warned. "We are not going to have the luxury of just going out and continuing to spend money. That's not going to happen, and it shouldn't.

"We've been horseshit, I've been horseshit, our organization has not had a good year," Leyland acknowledged.

"We're all in this together: the players, the manager, the coaches, the general manager—everybody except the owner, Mr. Ilitch, to be honest with you.

"Mr. Ilitch has been good about giving us the resources we need to be good," Leyland continued. "But a couple of those resources got hurt. And a couple haven't worked out.

"We've got some work to do. I know it sounds major, but I don't think it's as major as everybody thinks. It's not like we're starting from scratch. We've got a lot of nice pieces.

"Could we have a quick turnaround? Absolutely," he said. "We have basically a solid nucleus. We'll be pretty good next year."

*   *   *   *

Gosh, when you look at it, this has been the alpha-omega season. The beginning and the end were ugly, and somewhere in between we were okay.

I'm not making excuses for the way we've played in September. We've been bad. We've been a bad, ugly, underachieving baseball team. We've been uninspired and not very well coached.

Having said all that, we are not as bad as we have played this last month. But we certainly showed our weaknesses during the first month of the season and during the last month.

I kept thinking somebody in our bullpen would step up and establish themselves as *the guy*, as a legitimate late-inning reliever. I thought somebody would take advantage of the situation. But that just hasn't happened. We really haven't had anybody do that. I didn't anticipate that. I thought there was enough talent down there that somebody would step up and take advantage of the situation, but nobody has. I don't think anybody in our bullpen, including Fernando Rodney, can honestly say that they have done that.

It's been the same story all season. When we score five or more runs, we're usually okay. But nobody is ever going to win a pennant that way. You've got to win games 4–3 and 3–2 and 2–1, too.

We've had a share of losses when the scores have been big. And we've lost a lot of games, a lot of games, when the scores have been low.

SEPTEMBER 25, 2008
DETROIT, MI

Curtis Granderson belted a key seventh-inning home run—one of five homers by the Tigers this afternoon—to help end another six-game losing streak and spoil the Cinderella Tampa Bay Rays' champagne party, 7–5.

Today's win marked the 45th time the Tigers, who trailed 1–0 in the first inning, have come from behind to win a game this year.

Everyone expected the Tigers would be a team that simply overpowered the opposition, a team that would jump out in front by scoring a ton of runs and then stay there.

In fact, the opposite has been true. The Tigers lead the major leagues in come-from-behind wins.

However, as welcome as today's win was, it did nothing to ease the Tigers' pain.

"This year hasn't just been disappointing, this has been unbelievably disappointing," Jim Leyland admitted as the soul-searching continued at Comerica Park.

"We're embarrassed, and we should be—all of us. If we're not, there's something wrong.

"I'm embarrassed, Dave [Dombrowski] is embarrassed, the players should be embarrassed, and I think the fans are embarrassed.

"I'm embarrassed by our performance but not by any lack of effort," the manager continued. "I haven't seen one guy dog it. I haven't seen one guy not giving effort.

"We're trying; I don't see anyone who is not trying. Nobody here has quit—nobody. Everybody is doing the best they can do to play out a disappointing year.

"But is the mental edge the same? Is the atmosphere the same? No, it's not," Leyland acknowledged.

"It's different when you're 20 games over .500 than when you're 20 games under. Is your heart in it exactly the same way? No, it's not."

As Granderson continues to improve against left-handed pitching and cut down on his strikeouts, Leyland envisions a day when his talented center fielder, because of his power, will bat in the middle of the lineup.

However, that is not going to happen any time soon. The Tigers can't afford to move Granderson out of the leadoff position until they can find a suitable speedster to replace him.

. . . .

Forty-five come-from-behind wins? I wasn't even aware of that statistic. I had no idea we had come from behind to win that many games. But I think it's very important to make that fact known. That is the character of this ballclub; it never gives in.

I think that's a testament to Jim Leyland and his desire to keep competing, no matter what the circumstances. I think the players feed off that. I think we all realize we have a responsibility to play the game correctly and keep trying to win as many games as we can.

Sometimes that's hard to do when you have a veteran team like we do. Most of these guys have long-term guaranteed contracts. They don't need to go on a September salary drive the way younger players or players who don't have guaranteed contracts sometimes do. When you have a young team with a lot of players who are trying to establish themselves as major leaguers, sometimes it's a little easier to keep guys motivated at this time of the year. Most of these guys don't need to prove that they belong in the big leagues. They've already proven that.

But I haven't seen any major instances this year of a player just punching the clock or putting in his time. These guys still come out to the park early, they still get in their extra work, and they still prepare to win every night. They're a very professional team.

That's the only thing we can control at this point in the season: playing good baseball every day. That, to me, is an important part of the equation, looking ahead to next year. If that wasn't the case, I would say we would be in trouble for next season and in the years to follow.

But the competitive nature is there. There is a very prevalent feeling in this clubhouse every day that we can go out and beat the other team. To me, that really is the only thing that matters.

As for Curtis Granderson, I believe he is going to continue to improve every year, even though his numbers might not always say that. He's a kid who always wants to get better. That's the great thing about watching Curtis grow. He's learning to relax more, he's less nervous, and he's chasing fewer pitches out of the strike zone.

I predict, by the time Curtis is finished playing for the Tigers, he's going to be hitting somewhere in the middle of the lineup. But I like him in the leadoff role right now for our ballclub. I like him there until we can find someone who can really burn it.

Curtis creates problems for the opposing team from the first pitch on. He's a guy who can put you up, 1–0, with one swing of his bat. And he's a guy who can be on third base after two pitches. If you walk him, he can steal on you. If you pitch to him, he can beat you with a big hit. He can beat you with a home run, and he can beat you with a stolen base.

Guys like that are hard to find. When Curtis hits a ball in the gap or down the line, everybody on our team gets excited. You can feel it on the bench. Curtis is the fuel that runs our engine. And you can't be putting kerosene into an expensive car.

SEPTEMBER 26, 2008
DETROIT, MI

Owner Mike Ilitch, who has remained conspicuously out of sight all season, showed up at Comerica Park late this afternoon to pose for the annual team picture.

As an aspiring young ballplayer in the Tigers' minor-league farm system more than a half-century ago, Ilitch dreamed of someday playing in the World Series. Now, at 79, his goal is to own a world-championship baseball team.

Ilitch, who—along with just about everyone else—thought this was going be that dream year, admitted today he has been "humbled" by this summer's inexplicable collapse and hinted that changes in personnel are coming. He warned it may actually take a year or more before the Tigers can again contend.

"I know we'll be okay in a year or a year and a half, but I'm a little worried about next year," admitted Ilitch. "We've got a big job in front of us. A real big job.

"I just want to get back to where I thought we were, and that was competing with Boston and all the good teams—that's my goal, personally.

"We paid the price for miscalculating so deeply," Ilitch acknowledged. "I don't want to go through that again.

"I feel there were a lot of mistakes made. I didn't foresee all the holes we had. In my wildest dreams, I didn't anticipate that. I thought we had a nice, solid foundation that we were going to build from and keep the ballclub up, contending all the time. It didn't work out.

"We've got to level off now and have a reanalysis of who our real core players are and who we're going to keep," Ilitch continued. "I'm more concerned with getting the team in shape and seeing who we have and who are the real Detroit Tigers.

"We've got to look at each area and see what needs to be repaired. This cost us a little bit of time, maybe a year or a year and half. All the areas have failed.

We have to get ourselves restructured and correct all the mistakes that were made. We're not in a normal business. Anything can happen.

"Once we get that established, we can move forward," he added. "We're going to work like the dickens to get it back."

Gary Sheffield, back in the lineup after serving a four-game suspension for charging the mound and igniting that brawl in Cleveland a week ago, homered in both the first and the eighth innings tonight as the Tigers again topped playoff-bound Tampa Bay, 6–4.

Sheffield's two home runs gave him 19 for the year and 499 in his career, resulting in a Comerica Park curtain call and prompting a phone call from Sheffield to his uncle and childhood hero, former big-league pitcher Dwight Gooden, inviting him to come immediately to Detroit in case Gary connects for No. 500 tomorrow night.

Two months ago, as Sheffield continued to struggle to come back from off-season shoulder surgery, there was speculation the Tigers might cut him loose and eat the $14 million remaining on his contract for next year.

But the zing is back in his bat, and both Sheffield and the Tigers are now looking forward to next season.

·　·　·　·

I'm not going to change what I have said all along about Gary Sheffield: if he's healthy, he is still a very dangerous hitter.

The one thing I would encourage him to do is make a few adjustments. We all have to do that as we get older. Gary has always been a dead-pull hitter, which is fine. That is how he is going to be remembered, and that is how he is going to go into the Hall of Fame. But now that he's healthy, it's a lot easier for him to use the whole field. And he has started to do that a little more lately. I would encourage him to continue to do that.

This winter, for the first time in several years, Gary is not facing surgery or worrying about rehab. This year, he can go home, take a few weeks off to rest, and then start working out again. That's important because, at his age, he needs to shut it down—mentally and physically—for a good four to six weeks. And in past winters, because of surgery or rehab, Gary hasn't been able to do that.

But Gary is a hard worker. If he wasn't a hard worker, he wouldn't still be playing. His age and all of the surgeries he has had wouldn't allow him to do that. This guy has a lot of pride. He's extremely talented, and his concentration has always been there.

He can be a big RBI guy for us next year if his health is there. As you get older, it gets harder to play this game—especially if you're not healthy. At 25 you can get by when you don't feel so good. But at 40, that ain't gonna work.

Even at the age of 40, I think Gary could have a big year for us—if his health allows him to do that.

SEPTEMBER 27, 2008
DETROIT, MI

The retooling has begun.

In an effort to improve the Tigers' defense, which was too often deplorable this year, Brandon Inge will return to third base full-time next season, and Carlos Guillen will change positions for the third time in 12 months, moving from third base to left field in 2009.

The Tigers have made 113 errors this season, second-worst in the American League.

The moves—which were first suggested by Guillen himself back in April when he and Miguel Cabrera swapped positions—with Cabrera moving from third base to first—will mean the Tigers now have to find a new No. 1 catcher, either on the free-agent market or through a trade, and decide what to do with home-run-hitting Marcus Thames, who shared left-field duties this season, first with Jacque Jones and later with rookie Matt Joyce.

"I think this is the best thing for Inge and the best thing for the team," Jim Leyland explained tonight after the Tigers topped the worst-to-first Tampa Bay for the third day in a row, 4–3. "I'm not going to go into details, but I think we'll be better off."

Inge, who reluctantly resumed his old role as the Tigers' regular catcher at midseason when they traded Pudge Rodriguez and tried to put the best possible spin on the situation, was delighted by the latest change. Inge's heart was never truly into catching—and Leyland realized that.

"When [Leyland] called me into his office a week or so ago, he said, 'You're going to be my third baseman next year,'" Inge recalled.

"I was sitting in my chair and I [was] thinking, *Don't start smiling, don't start jumping around like a little kid*. But I couldn't help myself. I was smiling like a little kid."

After losing his job at third base to Cabrera, Inge initially balked at returning behind the plate to back up Rodriguez this year. But by the time the Tigers traded Rodriguez to the Yankees on July 30, Inge was resigned to the fact that he would be the team's every-day catcher in 2009.

When Leyland began playing Inge at third again this month in order to take a look at rookie catcher Dusty Ryan, the Tigers and their fans were reminded of what they had been missing on the left side of the infield this year.

Guillen admitted he isn't certain just how good a left fielder he will be next season.

"Who knows? Everybody thought I was going to win a Gold Glove at first base, too—and I looked like shit at first base," Guillen admitted.

"But I think Brandon Inge might be the best third baseman who ever played the game," said the former shortstop–turned–first baseman–turned–third baseman–now turned left fielder.

"Results, that's what this game is all about," Guillen added. "If you don't get good results with one lineup, you have to try something else.

"You can't keep waiting, waiting, waiting. Pull the trigger."

When the Tigers report to Lakeland for spring training, the position players will all know what their roles are.

"There will be no hanky-panky issues about who will play where," Leyland promised, referring to the uncertainty that swirled around Inge and others this past spring. "We were in a little bit of disarray this spring.

"Everybody needs to know what their position is. And everybody will know where they're playing and what to expect. Trust me when I tell you, things will be a little more back to normal next spring. There won't be any f*cking around. We won't be tinkering with stuff."

•   •   •   •

I think, more than anything else, those two changes are going to make our pitching better next year, because they're going to make our defense better. And whatever we can do to make our pitching better is the right thing to do right now.

In the case of Brandon Inge at third base, it was a matter of realizing you don't really miss what you have until it's gone. It's sort of like when I'm away from my wife for a couple of weeks because of this job. It's not that I don't appreciate my wife when she's in front of me and I see her every day, but I appreciate her even more when I'm on the road with the Tigers and she's not there.

That was the case with Brandon Inge. He's so good that whoever we put at third base in his place, as good as they may be, doesn't rise to the level Inge does when he's at third.

Obviously, the biggest fear is, is Brandon Inge going to offensively be the hitter he has been for the last two years— or is he going to be the hitter he was in 2006? We're hoping he can get close to what he was in '06. If he can, we'll be okay.

If Brandon drives in 75 runs next season, it will be like he has really driven in 100. That's how good he is at third base. That's how many runs he's going to prevent.

And I think Carlos Guillen will be the best left fielder we have had since I've been here. I don't know who the last good left fielder the Tigers had was, but I think people will be pleasantly surprised at how athletic Carlos will be out there. He's going to throw well, his footwork is not going to be an issue, and he can track balls fine. And I think, physically, it should be better for him. Left field can be—although not always—less stressful than playing the infield. So Carlos should be able to play more games next year. What you're going to see is a guy who looks pretty comfortable and pretty darn natural playing the outfield.

SEPTEMBER 28, 2008
DETROIT, MI

The Tigers' dismal pitching, third-worst in the American League this season, cost pitching coach Chuck Hernandez and bullpen coach Jeff Jones their jobs today.

Following an 8–7, 11-inning loss to Tampa Bay, in which, appropriately, the bullpen blew yet another game, Jim Leyland confirmed the rumors that had been making the rounds of the Tigers' clubhouse since late morning.

"I feel terrible about it," admitted an emotional Leyland, who said he arrived at the decision to let the two coaches go following a meeting with Tigers president/GM Dave Dombrowski on Tuesday. "I've had a knot in my stomach all week.

"That's one of the unfortunate things about a situation like this," Leyland said. "Sometimes things don't work, and somebody has to pay the price.

"Next year, at this time, it could be me," Leyland admitted.

In 2006 the Tigers rode their pitching staff, the best in the American League, all the way to the World Series. This year, that pitching was the third-worst in the AL, and it has taken them straight to the basement.

Leyland hated to have to make scapegoats out of two of his coaches. "I don't fire coaches," he said. But the collapse of the Tigers' pitching staff, in a season in which the team's payroll reached a record $139 million, made it impossible for Leyland to save the two men.

"It's tough because I know I'm partially to blame for this," admitted pitcher Justin Verlander, whose 11–17 record and 4.84 ERA was, in fact, largely to blame for the dismissal of Hernandez.

Despite the Tigers' dismal performance this season, 40,373 showed up at Comerica Park today for the home finale—not to boo, but to say good-bye.

That brought the total attendance for the year to a franchise-record 3,202,645.

. . . .

I just can't say enough about our fans and the way they've stuck with us this year. It's been amazing. Comerica Park was almost sold out for nearly every game all year, and that is a testament to how loyal the Detroit fans are and how much they want to see the Detroit Tigers succeed.

I know the Detroit fans are disappointed. We're all disappointed this year. But the Detroit fans have seen the character of this ballclub. They've seen that, even though we've had huge failures in a lot of areas, this team really hasn't given up in any game this year.

Chapter 9

POSTMORTEM

"Just Short of Disastrous"

The Hindenburg, the Titanic, and the 2008 last-place Tigers. Take your pick.

Not even the most jaundiced cynic or the Tigers' staunchest critic expected this. It was a season from hell.

In a spring-training survey of nearly 500 major-league players, 45 percent of them picked the Tigers to win the 2008 World Series. Seldom have so many felt so strongly—and been so shockingly wrong.

The best team Mike Ilitch's money could buy didn't spend a day in first place. The team that was supposed to win 100 games won just 74.

The Murderers' Row lineup that was supposed to score 1,000 runs scored just 821 and was shut out a dozen times. On three other occasions, they scored 19 runs in a game. Go figure.

The team that was supposed to blow away the rest of the American League instead blew 28 would-be wins in the late innings.

The team that was supposed to waltz to the World Series instead walked 644 enemy batters.

There was nothing lovable about these losers. There was nothing beloved about these bums.

"I don't think we responded very good to what people were writing about us and saying about us," manager Jim Leyland admitted.

The Tigers' Dream Cruise to what Leyland calls "the promised land," crumbled faster than Tiger Stadium, the saintly old ball yard at the corner of Michigan and Trumbull, which finally succumbed to the wrecking ball this summer, even as its former tenants were falling apart a mile away at Comerica Park. The irony was inescapable.

Tigers owner Mike Ilitch opened the vault in 2008, shelling out a franchise record $139 million in salaries. What he bought was a dud.

No baseball owner ever spent so much money and received so few victories in return. Each of the Tigers' 74 wins cost Ilitch close to $1.88 million. No baseball team ever spent so much money and still finished last.

The gilded coach that was supposed to carry the Tigers to the postseason ball turned into a pumpkin.

It was a waste of time and money—both for long-suffering Tigers fans and for their 79-year-old owner.

"When you get paid big, you're supposed to play big and you're supposed to manage big," Leyland admitted.

"When you get a big contract, there is some accountability that goes along with that. When it doesn't happen, people have a right to call you on the carpet. If some people can't handle that, they've got a problem."

The Tigers sold 3,202,645 tickets this season—the most in franchise history. Suffice it to say, those folks got gypped.

"Facts are facts, and the fact is, we stunk," admitted Leyland, who failed to get the contract extension that he coveted. He will be fighting to save his job in 2009.

"With the year we had, I stunk. But I can tell you one thing: I'm not the Lone Ranger," Leyland added. "I can't grab wins off trees. We all stunk. I didn't manage good enough, and we didn't play good enough."

However, the real shame of the 2008 season was not those 28 blown saves, or the 12 times the Tigers sluggers were shut out, or the fact that Dontrelle Willis was 0-for-'08, or the injuries to Jeremy Bonderman and Joel Zumaya, or the disappointment of Gary Sheffield and Edgar Renteria, or the decline of Todd Jones and Kenny Rogers, or those 644 walks.

No, the real shame of this lost summer was the fact that, in spite of all of their shortcomings, the American League Central still could have been—and still should have been—the Tigers' for the taking. And they knew it.

The Chicago White Sox and Minnesota Twins didn't blow the Tigers out of the water. They sunk themselves.

"We found out how hard it is to win," Leyland admitted. "We underachieved without question. Everybody in uniform did."

There were no century-old curses, no black cats, no billy goats to blame. The 2008 Tigers were their own worst enemies.

On those occasions when they did get good pitching, they usually didn't hit. When they hit, they usually didn't pitch. Other times, it was their defense that let them down.

"If you sum it up, pitching and defense are the name of the game," Leyland said. "And we weren't very good at either one. That's not pointing fingers; that's a fact.

"Throw stones at the whole team," Leyland added. "There are no individuals to throw stones at.

"We just didn't play good enough. We didn't manage good enough. We didn't coach good enough.

"Maybe I should have had some magical words. Maybe I didn't rub their tummies right or something."

The Tigers got off on the wrong foot in April, shockingly losing their first seven games and 10 of their first 12. And they never got back on their feet.

"Losing is the same thing as winning—when it starts happening, it snowballs on you," Leyland said.

Major League Baseball introduced instant replay to the grand ol' game in 2008. But the Tigers didn't need a replay to know why the most promising, the most anticipated season in their occasionally glorious 108-year history went so horribly awry.

"What went wrong? It's not rocket science. Look at the f*cking numbers! We won 74 games. That's the biggest number," Leyland declared.

"We were toward the bottom in pitching. We were toward the bottom in defense. That's what wins games: pitching and defense. Look at our walks. That's a disgrace. Not to mention the fact that we got shut out 12 times.

"We have a great product," Leyland continued. "We just didn't give a great performance. We had a year where nothing went right for us. Most of that, you can put on my shoulders. It starts with me. I'll take the blame."

The Tigers never got more than three games above .500. They never got closer to the lead than a one-day tie for second place, a game and a half back.

For the eighth year in a row, and the 14th time in the past 15 seasons, the Tigers lost more ballgames than they won after the midseason All-Star break.

In their defense, they were plagued by injuries—to Curtis Granderson, to Gary Sheffield, to Jeremy Bonderman, to Joel Zumaya, to Fernando Rodney, and to Todd Jones. One of their five intended starters, Dontrelle Willis, didn't win a game.

"We fell into a trap where we had too many cop-outs this season instead of taking care of our own business," Leyland explained.

"All the expectations—we fell into that trap. It was there for us, and we kind of used it."

Looking ahead, Leyland had one word of advice for his players in 2009: "Produce!"

Leyland continued, "Sooner or later, you've got to do the job. This is not a threat or anything, but people have to step it up.

"We've been a huge disappointment. We're under fire because of the year we've had and that's totally understandable. The days of babysitting and milking along are over.

"Do the job, or we'll get somebody else," warned Leyland, "If you're in the lineup, get a hit. If you're pitching, get somebody out.

"The best guys will be pitching, and the best guys will be playing next season. And I don't care what the names are, I can promise you that.

"We've been pretty nice about things around here, but I'm tired of worrying about guys being sensitive," he said. "I don't want to hear any whining or whispering. That's bullshit."

Leyland's will not be the only job that is on the line in '09.

With five weeks to go in the season and the Tigers just one game under .500, Leyland talked openly about wanting to manage for five more years and about asking his boss, president and general manager Dave Dombrowski, for a one-year extension on his contract, which is set to expire at the end of the 2009 season.

Just one year ago, Leyland rejected Dombrowski's offer of a two-year extension through 2010 insisting upon adding one year to his original three-year deal that he signed in 2006—with the understanding the two men would meet following the 2008 season to discuss adding another year to the manager's contract. But during the final five weeks of the '08 season, the Tigers lost 23 of their last 33 games

"I'd be embarrassed to ask for an extension right now," Leyland admitted as the Tigers limped toward the finish line.

However, the day after the '08 ordeal ended, Leyland, who had returned home to Pittsburgh following the final game, told a Detroit radio station he was "disappointed" Dombrowski had not offered him an extension through the 2010 season.

"I understand…well, maybe I don't understand," Leyland said during the radio interview. "But I can live with that. I'm sure Dave knows that I'm very disappointed, which I am.

"I don't want an option. I don't want a buyout. I want a contract, and I will try and earn another contract next year. I want to manage the Tigers. I have every intention of managing the Tigers. And I think I deserve to manage the Tigers. Overall, we've actually done pretty well.

"But if you're not wanted, you're not wanted," Leyland said. "I don't want to be anywhere I'm not wanted.

"I made it perfectly clear that I wanted to manage the Tigers. I think we had a great year [in 2006]. I think we had a good year [in 2007]. And then we had one disastrous year [in 2008]. I'll take my share of the blame for it.

"But," Leyland added, "you can put several people up on a dartboard, and if you threw a dart, you'd probably hit the right guy. We were all guilty.

"Let's face up to the music here. We didn't do the job, including me. At the head of the class. Did not do the job. Simple. There's no ifs, butts, and all that kind of stuff."

Leyland, a pack of Marlboros never far from his side, will be back on the bench in 2009—at a salary of $4 million a year, one of the highest of any manager in baseball.

"I think if I do a good job next year, I'll be extended," he predicted, optimistic as always.

"If I don't, I'll be fired."

. . . .

To sum up this season, I would say it was just short of disastrous. Frustrating, disappointing, disastrous—you can use any adjective you'd like, and it would probably be apropos. I have never been on a team that underachieved like this one did.

The thing about a baseball season is, you cannot hide your inefficiencies. You just cannot do it. Over the course of a 162-game season, those inefficiencies are going to constantly show themselves. And they did for us this season.

Statistically, obviously, our pitching was disappointing. The combination of our walks, our runs allowed, and our ERA—no team is going to win a division with the numbers that we put up in those three categories. And our bullpen, we blew 28 saves. That's a bad combination.

Looking back at our season statistically, for our club to have even been within earshot of contending, the way we were at the beginning of August when we were two games over .500 and in third place, was pretty amazing.

But for us to have gotten back into the race, after the way we started, we would have needed a good winning streak. And you can't have a winning streak like that without good starting pitching. You just can't do it.

The offensive numbers most of our guys put up this season aren't that bad at all. In many cases, they're about what we hoped for or expected. But no offense can carry a major-league baseball team for weeks or months. That's just not going to happen. You need good pitching, especially good starting pitching.

If you look back at 2006 and at the first part of 2007, we won a lot of ballgames 4–3 or 3–2. In 2006 our starters usually gave us six or seven innings. We didn't have to bring in two guys who had been released by other clubs to pitch the seventh inning the way we did on occasion this year.

In '06 we pitched well, we caught the ball okay, and we had enough offense to find ourselves in the World Series. It's not complicated. You just look like a better ballclub when you pitch well. That's the way it works. When you pitch better, you hit better and you play better defense. Those things go hand-in-hand.

When you're getting good pitching, you know that moving that runner over to second base in the middle innings instead of trying to drive him in by yourself, means something.

Good pitching has a way of relaxing the whole ballclub. We have to get better pitching next year; it's as simple as that.

Our offense has to share in the blame, too. Individually, guys like Miguel Cabrera and Magglio Ordonez and Placido Polanco had good years. But we were shut out 12 times this year. Nobody would have guessed that coming into this season.

We have to do better on both sides of the ball next year— pitching and hitting. We have to get better on defense, too. That will make our pitching better. If you're a pitcher and you know that if you make a good pitch you're going to get an out because the guys in the field are going to make the play behind you instead of letting the ball get past a glove somewhere, you have a tendency to throw more balls in the strike zone.

Everything in baseball is predicated around your pitching staff. As your pitching goes, so goes your offense. I really believe that. As a hitter, if you can grind out at-bats and know that you don't have to score five or six runs every night in order to win a ballgame, it tends to relax you. And we certainly did not have a shutdown year by our pitching staff.

What we hope to do during the off-season is remedy those things, those inefficiencies, that hurt us this year. But if you try to put a Band-Aid over them, they're just going to leak again next season. So hopefully we'll have some real surgical answers that will make us competitive next year.

When your best pitcher, Justin Verlander, doesn't even pitch .500 ball and has a 4.84 ERA, and you lose a pitcher like Jeremy Bonderman and a reliever like Joel Zumaya, and a lot of other guys like Curtis Granderson and Carlos Guillen get hurt, it all adds up. When you look at it that way, this season sort of makes sense, I guess. Sort of.

But when you look at the chasm between the expectations that we had coming into this season and the way we played and the disappointment at where we ended up, that gap is as wide as it has ever been for any team that I've ever been a part of.

This is a good ballclub. We've got some talented guys in the lineup. If we can figure out a way to extend our starters for another inning or so next season and figure out a way not to lose games late, I think this ballclub will look totally different than it did this year.

It doesn't matter to me if you finish 10 games under .500 or 20 games over .500. To me, the most important thing is how you compete. You can have a lot of talent on your ballclub, but if you don't have that competitive ingredient, you are not going to win. Believe me, I've been on teams like that.

To me, what matters is: What kind of attitude do you have when you show up at the ballpark? How much do you want to beat the other team? I think that is the most important thing. If you do that, most times your record is going to speak for itself, provided you pitch well and you stay healthy. That's my caveat. We didn't pitch well this year, and we had some injuries.

Do I think we'll be picked to win the American League Central in 2009? No, I don't. But we certainly shouldn't find ourselves in last place again.

AFTERWORD

By Carlos Guillen

This may have been the hardest year of my career.

We have to learn from what happened this year. We have to recognize the things that we have to do better in order to be a championship team.

Results. That's all I care about: winning. You have to play to win; you can't play not to lose. That was what happened to us this year. We were playing not to lose because we had too many expectations. You can't be thinking ahead to October when it's only April.

Next year, we've got to change that attitude, not from the first game but right from the first day of spring training.

We've got to be winners. We don't have to be heroes. I think, maybe, this season, too many guys were trying to be heroes.

To me, the hero is not the guy who gets the base hit to win the game. The hero is the guy who scores the winning run from second base with two outs on that hit.

It wasn't that we weren't trying to win every night. The players played hard every game, every day. We played like crap—but we tried. We knew something was wrong, but we didn't know how to fix it. You have to take a season one game at a time. You have to win the first one, then you think about what is going to happen tomorrow. You've got to take the season day-by-day, pitch-by-pitch, out-by-out.

We knew we had a good team this year. Everybody said, "Look at this team." Everybody was comparing our lineup to everybody else. The media called us "Murderers' Row." I think that got into everybody's heads. The players, the coaches, the manager, everybody. It got into the heads of the fans and the media, too. That put a lot of extra pressure on us because of the expectations.

But you don't win games in the newspapers; you win games on the field.

You never know what's going to happen. Certainly, nobody expected us to have a season like the one we had.

You've got to play with passion. You've got to play with heart. And you've got to have fun, to enjoy yourself.

When you go home every night and your wife asks, "What happened in the game?" and you have to say, "We lost," or when you call your wife from the road and you

Team leader Carlos Guillen, who moves to left field in 2009—his fourth position in three years—was the lone Tiger on the 2008 American League All-Star team. "The media called us 'Murderers' Row'—I think that got into everybody's head," Guillen observed. "But you don't win games in the newspaper. You win games on the field."

have to keep saying "We lost tonight," that is no fun. If you can go home every night or call your wife and say, "We won again tonight!" that makes a big difference.

We've got talent here. We've got all these big names. But we didn't enjoy this year because there was too much expectation. I don't think we had fun, right from the first day. When you don't win, you're not having fun. When we got off to that awful start, it made things worse.

Sometimes when you're under a lot of pressure, you don't think right. You're just trying to make it stop. You're just trying to make something happen. You're trying too hard. And when you do that, it's not going to happen. Next year, right from the first day of spring training, we've got to have fun.

Everybody talks about our bullpen. But to me, the problem this year was our starting pitching. Think back to what happened to us in 2006 when we went to the World Series. Every starting pitcher threw seven innings almost every time out.

This year, our starting pitchers were only going five innings, and we blew out the bullpen early in the season. How many times did the starting pitchers go seven innings? Not very often. So we had to bring in our relief pitchers in the sixth inning or sometimes even the fifth inning. Sometimes they had to pitch two innings when they should have only pitched one. That put too much pressure on our bullpen.

A lot of guys in the bullpen did a good job early in the year, but we blew them out because we had to use them too much. I know our pitchers were trying to do their best, but we blew 28 saves this year. That shouldn't happen. That shows our hitters were doing their job most of the time. I'm not pointing fingers at anybody. We are all to blame, including me.

But to me, the key to any baseball season is pitching. This game is all about pitching. Pitching and defense. Those are the two most important things. Hitting is nice. You need to have that, too. But you have to have good pitching in order to win.

We had a good lineup this year. We had Miguel Cabrera, we had Magglio Ordonez, we had Edgar Renteria, we had Placido Polanco, we had me. But you don't win with hitting. Your hitters play every day. They get tired. They go into slumps. But your starting pitchers, they only have to pitch once every five days. The starting pitchers have to go longer next year. The starting pitchers have to be more consistent.

We have to stay healthy next year, too. Almost everybody got hurt at some point this season. Gary Sheffield was hurt. Magglio got hurt. Polly got hurt. I got hurt. We had too many injuries. You're not going to win like that.

A little bit more speed would help, too, so that in the late innings we could sometimes score a run without getting a base hit, or just with a single. You need to be able to do that. When you get a guy on first base, you need to be able to get him to second without a sacrifice bunt. Good teams win with speed. That's how you put pressure on the defense and put pressure on the pitcher. You force them to make a mistake.

We need to be more positive. We need to work a little harder. We need to concentrate a little bit more. Every player, including me. We need to be more consistent. That's the way you win championships: with consistency. If we want to win, that's what we've got to do as a team. We've got to be more consistent.

And we have to count on what we've got. The guys who are here, they are our team. We don't want to be counting on the birds in the air. Because you never know if you're going to catch that bird or not.

We brought Armando Galarraga up from the minor leagues this year. He did a good job for us. Nobody expected somebody to come up from the minor leagues and pitch like he did.

But when you start counting on the birds in the air, like we sometimes did this year, that's when you get into trouble.

We didn't start the season with everybody healthy. Curtis Granderson started the season on the disabled list. Joel Zumaya was out. Fernando Rodney was hurt. And we were counting on Dontrelle Willis. To me, that changed everything. On any night, we didn't know who was going to be available in the bullpen before we could get to our closer, Todd Jones. To me, injuries were another key to this season. That was why we got off to such a bad start.

When we have Curtis Granderson in the lineup, when he gets on base, it's good for Placido Polanco, it's good for Magglio Ordonez, its good for Miguel Cabrera, it's good for everybody. Everybody can have a better season with Curtis in there. Because he gets on base, he scores a lot of runs, he hits a lot of triples, he sets the pace for the rest of the lineup.

We've got to learn from what happened to us this year. This team lost 119 games in 2003, but those guys learned from that. And we went to the World Series three years later.

That's baseball.

About the Authors

 ANDY VAN SLYKE is the Detroit Tigers' first base, outfield and base-running coach. During his playing days, primarily with the St. Louis Cardinals and Pittsburgh Pirates, Andy, a first-round draft pick in 1979, was a three-time All-Star and winner of five Gold Gloves for defensive excellence and two Silver Slugger Awards as the top offensive outfielder in the National League. He twice finished fourth in National League MVP balloting.

 JIM HAWKINS is the baseball writer and columnist for the *Oakland (Michigan) Press*. He began covering the Tigers as a 25-year-old rookie reporter in 1970. He returned to the beat in 2006 when the team's games suddenly became meaningful again. This is his sixth book, his fourth on the Tigers, including biographies of former Tiger stars Mark Fidrych (*Go, Bird, Go*) and Ron LeFlore (*Breakout*) and *The Detroit Tigers Encyclopedia*.